CAMBRIDGE LIBRARY COLLECTION

Books of enduring scholarly value

Cambridge

The city of Cambridge received its royal charter in 1201, having already been home to Britons, Romans and Anglo-Saxons for many centuries. Cambridge University was founded soon afterwards and celebrated its octocentenary in 2009. This series explores the history and influence of Cambridge as a centre of science, learning, and discovery, its contributions to national and global politics and culture, and its inevitable controversies and scandals.

St John's College, Cambridge

St John's College, Cambridge, founded in 1511 by Lady Margaret Beaufort, is one of the largest colleges in the University, and is home to one of Cambridge's famous landmarks, the Bridge of Sighs. The author, R. F. Scott, was Master of the College from 1908 until his death in 1933. This history, first published in 1907, covers the period from its foundation, on the ancient site of the hospital of St John the Evangelist, to the start of the twentieth century. Each chapter is dedicated to a different century, and the book finishes with an account of the contemporary social life of the college. Copiously illustrated throughout and with a comprehensive index, this book will appeal to anyone interested in Cambridge University and specifically to those fascinated by college life and history.

T0384503

Cambridge University Press has long been a pioneer in the reissuing of out-of-print titles from its own backlist, producing digital reprints of books that are still sought after by scholars and students but could not be reprinted economically using traditional technology. The Cambridge Library Collection extends this activity to a wider range of books which are still of importance to researchers and professionals, either for the source material they contain, or as landmarks in the history of their academic discipline.

Drawing from the world-renowned collections in the Cambridge University Library, and guided by the advice of experts in each subject area, Cambridge University Press is using state-of-the-art scanning machines in its own Printing House to capture the content of each book selected for inclusion. The files are processed to give a consistently clear, crisp image, and the books finished to the high quality standard for which the Press is recognised around the world. The latest print-on-demand technology ensures that the books will remain available indefinitely, and that orders for single or multiple copies can quickly be supplied.

The Cambridge Library Collection will bring back to life books of enduring scholarly value (including out-of-copyright works originally issued by other publishers) across a wide range of disciplines in the humanities and social sciences and in science and technology.

St John's College, Cambridge

ROBERT FORSYTH SCOTT

CAMBRIDGE UNIVERSITY PRESS

Cambridge, New York, Melbourne, Madrid, Cape Town, Singapore,
São Paolo, Delhi, Dubai, Tokyo

Published in the United States of America by Cambridge University Press, New York

www.cambridge.org
Information on this title: www.cambridge.org/9781108017947

© in this compilation Cambridge University Press 2010

This edition first published 1907
This digitally printed version 2010

ISBN 978-1-108-01794-7 Paperback

The College

Monographs

THE COLLEGE
MONOGRAPHS
Edited and Illustrated by
EDMUND H. NEW

TRINITY COLLEGE,
CAMBRIDGE
      W. W. ROUSE BALL.

ST. JOHN'S COLLEGE,
CAMBRIDGE
      R. F. SCOTT.

KING'S COLLEGE,
CAMBRIDGE
      C. R. FAY.

MAGDALEN COLLEGE,
OXFORD
      THE PRESIDENT.

NEW COLLEGE,
OXFORD
      A. O. PRICKARD.

MERTON COLLEGE,
OXFORD
      REV. H. J. WHITE.

Gateway

St John's Coll.

ST. JOHN'S COLLEGE

CAMBRIDGE

BY

ROBERT FORSYTH SCOTT

FELLOW AND SENIOR BURSAR
OF THE COLLEGE

ILLUSTRATED BY

EDMUND H. NEW

1907 : LONDON : J. M. DENT & CO.
NEW YORK : E. P. DUTTON & CO.

CONTENTS

CHAP.   PAGE

  I. THE COURTS AND BUILDINGS .   1

 II. SOME INTERIORS .   .   .   13

III. THE HOSPITAL OF ST. JOHN (CIRCA

       1135–1511)   35

 IV. THE FIRST CENTURY (1511–1612) . 40

  V. THE SECOND CENTURY (1612–1716) 52

 VI. THE THIRD CENTURY (1716–1815) 66

VII. THE CURRENT CENTURY . . 74

VIII. SOCIAL LIFE 86

INDEX 109

LIST OF ILLUSTRATIONS

The Entrance Gateway . . . *Frontispiece*

PAGE

Plan of College Buildings . . . x

Bag of Flowers ; detail of Carving over
    Entrance Gateway 3

The Second and Third Courts from the
    Screens 6

The Gatehouse from the Churchyard of All
    Saints 12

Monument of Hugh Ashton in the Chapel . 19

The Hall from the Second Court . . 24

Interior of the Library 34

The Old Bridge 41

The Hall and Chapel Tower from the Second
    Court 53

The College Arms (in the Third Court) . 58

The Chapel Tower from the River . . 67

The College Chapel from the Round Church 75

The New Court from Trinity College Bridge 87

The " Bridge of Sighs " . . . 98

Plan of St. John's College

Legend:
- 1510–1520
- 1598–1673
- 19th Cent.y

New Court 1825–31

Garden

R. Cam

Old Br.

Bridge of Sighs

Library

Third Ct. 1669–73

Master's Garden

Master's Lodging 1869

1884

Second Court 1598–1602

Comb.n Room

Chapel Court

Trinity College

Rebuilt 1774

Kitchen Hall

First Court 1510–20

Site of Old Ch.

Chapel 1864–9

St John's Street

Bridge St.

Ch.

N W S E

St. John's College

CHAPTER I

THE COURTS AND BUILDINGS

ST. John's College was founded in 1511, in pursuance of the intentions of the Lady Margaret Beaufort, mother of King Henry VII.

Approaching the College from the street we enter by the Great Gate. The gateway with its four towers is the best example of the characteristic Cambridge gate, and dates from the foundation of the College. It is built of red brick (the eastern counties marble), dressed with stone. The street front of the College to the right and left remains in its original state, except that after the old chapel and infirmary of the Hospital of St. John (to which allusion will be made hereafter) were pulled down, the north end was completed by a block of lecture rooms in 1869.

The front of the gate is richly decorated with heraldic devices, full of historical meaning and associations. The arms are those of the foundress; the shield, France (ancient) and England quarterly, was the royal shield of the period ; the bordure, gobonny argent and azure (the argent in the upper dexter compartment), was the " difference 'ᒾ of the Beauforts, and is only slightly indicated. The supporters, two antelopes, come from Henry VI. There is no crest above the shield, and heraldic rules are against its use by a lady, but on her seal the Lady Margaret used the Beaufort arms as above ensigned, with a coronet of roses and fleur-de-lis, out of which issues an eagle, displayed or ; and this device of coat and crest is used by the College. The arms on the gate are surrounded by badges, the Portcullis of the Beauforts, the Tudor, or Union, rose, each surmounted by a crown. Besides these we have daisies (marguerites), the badge of the Lady Margaret, and some flowers, which are not so easily identified. Certain vestments and embroideries, which belonged to the Lady Margaret, of which a list has been preserved, are described as " garnishede with sophanyes and my ladyes poisy," or, " with rede roses and syphanyes." The sophanye was an old English name for the Christmas rose, and there seems little doubt that these flowers on the gate are meant for Christmas roses. The carving on the right, under the portcullis, where these emblems seem to be growing out of something resembling a masonic apron, is very curious.

Above the gate are two sets of rooms,

The upper set has been used from the beginning as the Treasury or Muniment Room of the College; the set immediately above the arch is now an ordinary set of rooms. In this set resided, during his college career, Lord Thomas Howard, a son of the fourth Duke of Norfolk, after-

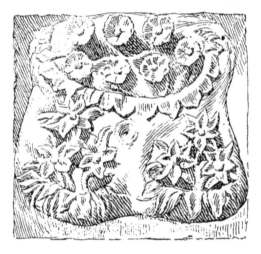

BAG OF FLOWERS OVER ENTRANCE GATEWAY

wards himself first Earl of Suffolk and Baron Howard de Walden. He fought against the Armada in 1588, and commanded the expedition to the Azores in 1591; the fame of Sir Richard Grenville of the *Revenge* has somewhat eclipsed that of his leader in the latter case; the reader may recall Tennyson's *Ballad of the Fleet*.

To the left of the gate it will be observed that five windows on the first floor are of larger size than the rest; this was the original position of the Library; the books were removed in 1616 to a room over the Kitchen, and later to the present Library. According to tradition Henry Kirke White, the poet, occupied, and died in, the rooms on the ground-floor next the tower; he lies buried in the old churchyard of All Saints', across the street.

Entering the gate the Hall and Kitchen face us, and preserve much of their original appearance. But right and left the changes have been great. The old Chapel was swept away in 1869—its foundations are marked out by cement; at this time the Hall was lengthened, and a second oriel window added. The range of buildings on the south was raised and faced with stone about 1775, when the craze for Italianising buildings was fashionable; it was then intended to treat the rest of the Court in like manner, but fortunately the scheme was not carried out.

If we walk along the south side of the Court we may notice on the underside of the lintel of G staircase the words, "Stag, Nov. 15, 1777." It seems that on that date a stag, pursued by the hunt, took refuge in the College, and on this staircase; the members of the College had just finished dinner when the stag and his pursuers entered. On the next staircase, F, there is a passage leading to the lane with the Kitchen Offices, this passage is sometimes known as "The Staincoat"; the passage leading from the Screens into the Kitchen is still sometimes called "The Staincoat," or "The Stankard." These curious names really mean the same thing. It appears that in times past a pole was kept, probably for carrying casks of beer, but on which the undergraduates seem also to have hoisted those of their number, or even servants, who had offended against the rules and customs of the College; this pole was called the Stang, and the place or passage in which it was kept the Stangate Hole, with the above variations or corruptions.

Reserving the Chapel for the present we pass through the Screens, the entrance to the Hall being on the right, to the Kitchen on the left. We enter the Second Court. This beautiful and stately Court was built between 1599 and 1600 (the date 1599 may be seen on the top of one of the water-pipes on the north side), the cost being in great part provided by Mary, Countess of Shrewsbury, a daughter of Sir William Cavendish by the celebrated Bess of Hardwick, and wife of Gilbert, seventh Earl of Shrewsbury. The original drawings for the Court, and the contract for its construction, almost unique documents of their kind, are preserved in the Library. The whole of the first floor on the north side was at first used as a gallery for the Master's Lodge; it is now used as a Combination Room. Over the arch of the gate on

the western side of the Court is a statue of
the Countess, with her shield (showing the
arms of Talbot and Cavendish impaled);
these were presented to the College by

VIEW FROM THE SCREENS

her nephew, William Cavendish, Duke of
Newcastle.

A pleasing view of the Court is got by
standing in the south-west corner and
looking towards the Chapel Tower, with
an afternoon sun the colouring and group-
ing of the buildings is very effective.

Passing through the arch we enter the
Third Court; this was built at various

6

times during the seventeenth century. On the north we have the Library, the cost of which was chiefly provided by John Williams, a Fellow of the College, successively Dean of Westminster, Bishop of Lincoln, and Archbishop of York; he was also Lord Keeper of the Great Seal to James I. As originally built the Library occupied the upper floor only, the ground-floor being fitted up as rooms for the accommodation of the Fellows and scholars, on a special foundation of Bishop Williams, but this lower part is now all absorbed into the Library. The southern and western sides of the Court were built between 1669 and 1674, some part of the cost being provided from College funds, the rest by donations from members of the College. On the last or southern pier of the arcade, on the west side of the Court, there are the two inscriptions : "Flood, Oct. 27, 1762," "Flood, Feb. 10, 1795," recording what must have been highly inconvenient events at the time.

The central arch on the western side of the Court has some prominence, and was probably intended from the first as the approach to a bridge. Towards the end of the seventeenth century Sir Christopher Wren was consulted on the subject, and a letter from him to the then Master, Dr. Gower, has been preserved. Sir Christopher's proposal was a curious one : he suggested that the course of the river Cam

7

should be diverted and carried in a straight line from the point where it bends near the Library of Trinity College. A new channel was to be dug, and a bridge built over this; the water was then to be sent down the new channel, and the old one filled up. He pointed out that this would give "a parterre to the river, a better access to the walks, and a more beautiful disposal of the whole ground." This scheme was, however, not carried out, but a stone bridge was built outside the range of the buildings on the site of an old wooden bridge, which then gave access to the grounds. This is the bridge which still exists; it was built, apparently from Wren's designs, under the superintendence of his pupil, Nicholas Hawksmoor. More than a century now passed before further building operations were undertaken. In 1825 the College employed Mr. Thomas Rickman and his partner, Mr. H. Hutchinson, to prepare designs for a new Court, with from 100 to 120 sets of rooms. This work was started in 1827, and completed in 1831. The covered bridge connecting the old and new parts of the College was designed by Mr. Hutchinson; it is popularly known as the "Bridge of Sighs." The style of this Court is Perpendicular Gothic. The site was unsuited for building operations, consisting mostly of washed and peaty soil; it had been known for generations as "the fishponds close." The modern concrete foundations were then unknown, and the plan adopted was to remove the peaty soil and to lay timber on the underlying gravel. On this an enormous mass of brickwork, forming vaulted cellars, was placed; this rises above the river level, and the rooms are perfectly dry. The total cost of the building was £78,000, most of which was provided by borrowing. The repayment, extending over a number of years, involved considerable self-denial on the Fellows of the College, their incomes being materially reduced for many years. Crossing the covered bridge and passing down the cloisters of the New Court, we enter the grounds by the centre gate; these extend right and left, being bounded on the east by the Cam, and separated from the grounds of Trinity by a ditch.

From the old, or Wren's, bridge over the Cam two parallel walks extend along the front of the Court; according to tradition the broader and higher was reserved for members of the College, the lower for College servants. At one time an avenue of trees extended from the bridge to the back gate, but the ravages of time have removed all but a few trees.

At the western end of the walk we have on the left the (private) Fellows' garden, known as "The Wilderness," an old-world pleasance, left as nearly as may be in a state of nature. Towards the end of the eighteenth century the

9

College employed the celebrated Mr. Lancelot ("capability") Brown to lay out the grounds and Wilderness. The plantation in the latter was arranged so as to form a cathedral, with nave, aisles, and transept, but here also old age and storms have brought down many of the trees. On the right, opposite to the Wilderness, there is an orchard, the subject of much legend. One popular story is that this orchard formed the subject of a bequest to "St. John's College," and that the testator, being an Oxford man, was held by the Courts to have intended to benefit the College in his own University. As a matter of prosaic fact, the orchard originally belonged to Merton College, Oxford, being part of the original gift of their founder, Walter de Merton, and it was acquired by St. John's College by exchange in the early years of the nineteenth century.

The long walk terminates in a massive gate with stone pillars, surmounted by eagles. Outside and across the road is the Eagle Close, used as the College cricket and football field.

The visitor in returning should cross the old bridge, thus getting a view of the Bridge of Sighs, and re-enter the College by the archway on the left.

The Gatehouse: St John's College

CHAPTER II

THE visitor has been conducted through the College without pausing to enter any of the buildings. We now retrace our steps to describe these parts of the College open to inspection. It must be understood that during a great part of the year the inspection of these interiors is subject to the needs of a large resident Society, and as a rule it is best to inquire at the gate for information as to the hours when these parts of the College are open.

The Chapel.

The present Chapel was built between the years 1863 and 1869, from the designs of Sir George Gilbert Scott; it was consecrated by the Bishop of Ely, 12th May 1869. As we approach it we see on the right the outline of the old Chapel, which had served the College and the Hospital which preceded it for something like six hundred years. This former Chapel was a building quite uniform and simple in appearance, filling the whole of the north side of the Court. Originally built to serve

13

the needs of the Hospital of St. John, it was
considerably altered when the College was
founded. Side Chantries were then, or
shortly afterwards, added. In early times
a good deal of the life of the College
centred in the Chapel, in addition to its
uses for worship. It was regarded as a
place in which the Society was formally
gathered together. In it the statutes, or
rules for the government of the Society,
were read at stated times, so that all might
become aware of the rule under which
they lived. The names of those who had
not discharged their College bills were
publicly read out by the Master. The
elections of the Master and of the Fellows
and Scholars were held within it; of this
practice the sole part that remains is the
election of a Master, which by the present
statutes must be held in the Chapel. The
scholastic exercises of Acts and Oppon-
encies, in which certain doctrines were
maintained and opposed, took place there.
The seal of the College was kept in the
vestry, and the sealing of documents took
place in the Ante-Chapel. Though documents are now sealed elsewhere, the stock
of wafers for the College seal is kept by the
Chapel Clerk.

The erection of a new Chapel for the
College was contemplated for about 200
years before it was carried out. Dr. Gunning, who was Master from 1661 to 1670,
afterwards successively Bishop of Chichester

and of Ely, left by his will the sum of £300 "to St. John's College, towards the beginning for the building for themselves a new Chapel." Gunning died in 1684, and in 1687 the College paid to Robert Grumbold the sum of £3 for "a new ground plott modell of the old and new designed Chappell." Nothing, however, came of the proposal at that time, though the idea seems always to have been before the Society.

Preaching on Commemoration Day (May 6), 1861, Dr. William Selwyn, Lady Margaret Professor of Divinity, and a former Fellow, pointing out that the College was celebrating "its seventh jubilee," just 350 years having passed since the charter was granted, pleaded earnestly for the erection of a larger Chapel. The matter was taken up, and in January 1862 Sir (then Mr.) George Gilbert Scott was requested "to advise us as to the best plans, in his opinion, for a new Chapel." The scheme grew, and in addition to the Chapel it was determined by the end of that year to have also a new Master's Lodge, and to enlarge the Dining Hall. It was then intended that the scheme should not involve a greater charge on the corporate funds of the College than £40,000. As a matter of fact, before the whole was carried out and paid for, the cost had risen to £97,641 ; of this £17,172 was provided for by donations from members of the College, the rest was met, partly out of capital, partly by a charge on the College revenues, which ran for many years.

The Chapel was built on a site to the north of the old Chapel, and through this site ran a lane from St. John's Street to the river. An Act of Parliament had to be obtained before this lane could be closed, and the consent of the borough was only given on condition that St. John's Street should be widened by pulling down a row of houses on its western side, and throwing their site into the street.

The foundation-stone of the new Chapel was laid on 6th May 1864 by Mr. Henry Hoare, a member of the College, and of the well-known banking firm. As originally designed the Chapel was to have had a slender *flèche* instead of a tower. This had been criticised, and Mr. Scott, the architect, designed the present tower; the additional cost being estimated at £5000. This Mr. Hoare offered to provide in yearly instalments of £1000, but had only paid two instalments when he died from injuries received in a railway accident. The finial on the last pinnacle of the tower was fixed on 13th December 1867 by Mr. (now Sir Francis) Powell, M.P. for the borough of Cambridge, and a former Fellow of the College; Mr. Powell was accompanied on that occasion by Professor John Couch Adams and the Rev. G. F. Reyner, the Senior Bursar of the College.

The new Chapel was, as we have said, opened in 1869, and the old Chapel then cleared away. The woodwork of the stalls had been transferred to the new Chapel, but most of the internal fittings were scattered. The ancient rood-screen stands in the church of Whissendine, in Rutlandshire, and the old organ-case in Bilton Church, near Rugby, and other parts of the fabric were dispersed ; it was perhaps inevitable. Sir Gilbert Scott's idea was that the new Chapel should be of the same period of architecture as the old, but it is absolutely different in design ; in the lover of things old there must always be a feeling of regret for what has gone. The mural tablets in the old Chapel were removed to the new Ante-Chapel, the slabs in the floor were left. It is worth noting that Eleazar Knox, a Fellow of the College, and one of the sons of John Knox, the famous Scotch Reformer, was buried in the Chapel in 1591. His elder brother, Nathanael Knox, was also a Fellow. To the north of the old Chapel, and bordering on the lane which has been mentioned, stood the Infirmary of the Hospital which preceded the College. This was originally a single long room, of which the eastern end formed an oratory. In this the poor and sick, for whose benefit the Hospital was founded, were received, and Mass said for them, and in their sight, as they lay in their beds. This Infirmary, after the foundation of the

College, was devoted to secular uses. For
some time it was used as a stable and
storehouse for the Master. Then later it
was fitted up with floors and turned into
chambers. It was approached by a tortuous
passage at the eastern end of the Chapel,
and was popularly known as the Labyrinth.
When the Infirmary was taken down a very
beautiful double piscina was found covered
up on the walls; this is preserved in the
new Chapel.

The new Chapel is built of Ancaster
stone, and is in the style of architecture
known as Early Decorated, which pre-
vailed about 1280, the probable date of the
Chapel of the Hospital. Sir Gilbert Scott
very skilfully made the most of the site, and
by the device of the transeptal Ante-Chapel
made full use of the space at his disposal.

At the springs of the outer arch of the
great door are heads of King Henry VIII.
and of Queen Victoria, indicating the date
of the foundation of the College and of the
erection of the Chapel. On the north side
of the porch is a statue of the Lady Margaret, and on the south one of John Fisher,
Bishop of Rochester.

The statues on the buttresses are those of
famous members of the College, or of its
benefactors. Those facing the Court are
William Cecil, Lord Burghley; Lucius
Carey, Viscount Falkland; John Williams,
Lord Keeper to James I.; Thomas Wentworth, Lord Strafford; William Gilbert,

author of *De Magnete*, in which the theory
of the magnetism of the earth was first
developed, and physician to Queen Elizabeth ; Roger Ascham, and the Countess of
Shrewsbury.

We enter the Ante-Chapel. This has a

MONUMENT OF HUGH ASHTON

stone-vaulted roof ; over the central bay the
tower is placed. On the south wall are
placed the arches from Bishop Fisher's
Chantry in the old Chapel. The monument with the recumbent figure is that of
Hugh Ashton, comptroller of the household

19

to the Lady Margaret, a prebendary and Archdeacon of York. He was buried in the old Chapel, and this tomb originally stood in a chantry attached thereto. He founded four fellowships and four scholarships in the College, the Fellows being bound to sing Mass for the repose of his soul. The carving on the tomb and on the finials of the railing around it include a rebus on his name, an ash-tree growing out of a barrel (ash-tun). On the north wall is a bust of Dr. Isaac Todhunter, the well-known mathematical writer ; on the western wall a tablet by Chantrey, to the memory of Kirke White, the poet, who died in College. He was buried in the chancel of the old Church of All Saints, which stood opposite to the College ; when the church was pulled down the tablet was transferred to the College Chapel. The statue is that of James Wood, sometime Master of the College, part of whose bequests went towards building the Chapel. On the east wall is an old brass to the memory of Nicholas Metcalfe, third Master of the College, the words *"vestras . . . preces vehementer expetit"* have been partly obliterated, probably during the Commonwealth. The roof of the Choir is of high pitch, of quadripartite vaulting in oak, and is decorated with a continuous line of full-length figures. In the central bay at the east end is our Lord in Majesty, the other bays contain figures illustrating the

Christian centuries. Owing to the deep colour of the glass in the windows, it is only on a very sunny day that the figures can be clearly discerned. The windows in the Choir have been given by various donors, the subjects being scenes from Scripture at which St. John was present; his figure robed in ruby and green will be seen in each. The five windows in the apse, the gift of the Earl of Powis, High Steward of the University, depict scenes from the Passion, Crucifixion, and Resurrection of Christ. In the apse is preserved the double piscina which was found covered up in the walls of the Infirmary, and removed by Sir G. G. Scott, with such repairs as were absolutely necessary. It is probably one of the oldest specimens of carved stonework in Cambridge.

The steps leading up to the Altar are paved with Purbeck, Sicilian, and black Derbyshire marbles. The spaces between the steps are decorated with a series of scriptural subjects in inlaid work in black and white marble, with distinctive inscriptions. The Altar is of oak, with a single slab of Belgian marble for its top. On the sides of the Altar are deeply carved panels; that in the centre represents the Lamb with the Banner, the other panels contain the emblems of the four Evangelists.

The organ stands in a special chamber on the north side; the carved front was not put in place till 1890. It was designed by

Mr. J. Oldrid Scott, a son of Sir Gilbert
Scott. In 1635 the famous Robert Dallam
of Westminster built a "paire of new
orgaines" for the College. The organ
has been repeatedly enlarged, altered, and
improved; it may be that some of Dallam's
work still remains, though this is uncertain.
The present organ is one of the best in
Cambridge; its tone throughout is uniformly beautiful.

The brass reading-desk was given to the
old Chapel by the Rev. Thomas Whytehead, a Fellow of the College; the pedestal
is copied from the wooden lectern in
Ramsay Church, Huntingdonshire; the
finials, which are there wanting, having
been restored, and the wooden desk replaced by an eagle.

As we return to the Ante-Chapel we
may note the great west window, repre-
senting the Last Judgment; this was given
by the Bachelors and Undergraduates of
the College. There are also windows in the
Ante-Chapel to the memory of Dr. Ralph
Tatham, Master of the College, and to the
Rev. J. J. Blunt, Lady Margaret Professor of Divinity.

The oil-painting which hangs on the
south wall of the Ante-Chapel near the
door—a Descent from the Cross—is by
Anthony Raphael Mengs. It was given to
the College in 1841 by the Right Hon.
Robert Henry Clive, M.P. for Shrop-
shire.

SOME INTERIORS

The Hall.

We enter the Hall from the Screens, between the First and Second Courts. The southern end is part of the original building of the College. It was at first about seventy feet long, with one oriel only, the old Combination Room being beyond it. When the new Chapel was built the Hall was lengthened, and the second oriel window added. The oak panelling is of the old "linen" pattern, and dates from the sixteenth century ; that lining the north wall, beyond the High Table, is very elaborately carved, being the finest example of such work in Cambridge. Within living memory all this oak work was painted green. The fine timbered roof has a lantern turret, beneath which, until 1865, stood an open charcoal brazier. From allusions in early documents it would appear that members of the Society gathered round the brazier for conversation after meals. In addition to its use as a dining-room, the Hall also served as a lecture-room, and for the production of stage plays. On these latter occasions it seems to have been specially decorated, for Roger Ascham, writing 1st October 1550, from Antwerp, to his brother Fellow, Edward Raven, tried to picture to him the magnificence of the city by saying that it surpassed all others which he had visited, as much as the Hall at St. John's, when

23

decorated for a play at Christmas, surpassed its appearance at ordinary times.

Many of the College examinations are held in the Hall, and in the days of the brazier, examinees were warned by their

The Hall, S͞t͞ John's College

Tutors not to sit too near the brazier; the comfort from the heat being dearly purchased by the drowsiness caused by the fumes of the charcoal.

Many interesting portraits hang on the walls. That of the foundress in the centre of the north wall is painted on wooden

panel, and is very old. She is flanked by
Lord Keeper Williams, and by Sir Ralph
Hare, K.C.B., both benefactors to the
College. Other noteworthy portraits are
those of Sir Noah Thomas, physician to
King George III., by Romney; William
Wordsworth, poet-laureate, by Pickersgill;
Professor John E. B. Mayor, by Herkomer;
Professor B. H. Kennedy, long headmaster
of Shrewsbury School, by Ouless; Professor
E. H. Palmer, Lord Almoner's Reader of
Arabic in the University, and a famous
oriental scholar, by the Hon. John Collier;
and Professor G. D. Liveing, by Sir George
Reid.

The shields in the windows are those of
distinguished members of the College, or
benefactors. The further oriel window has
busts of Sir John F. W. Herschel and Professor John Couch Adams.

The Combination Room.

We enter by the staircase at the north
end of the Hall. This was originally about
187 feet long, extending the whole length
of the Second Court, and was used as a
gallery in connection with the old Master's
Lodge. The ceiling dates from 1600, and
the panelling from 1603. In 1624 about
42 feet were sacrificed to obtain a staircase
and vestibule for the Library; the ceiling
can be traced right through. In the
eighteenth century partitions were put up,

dividing up the gallery into rooms. When the new Master's Lodge was built these partitions were removed, and the whole now forms two Combination Rooms.

In the oriel window on the south side is an old stained-glass portrait of Henrietta Maria, Queen of King Charles I. The tradition runs that the marriage articles between Prince Charles and Henrietta Maria were signed in this room; King James I. was at that time holding his Court in Trinity College.

A number of interesting portraits hang on the walls : George Augustus Selwyn, Bishop of New Zealand, afterwards of Lichfield, by George Richmond, R.A. ; a chalk drawing (also by Richmond) of William Tyrrell, Bishop of Newcastle, New South Wales; of Sir John Herschel and Professor J. C. Adams; of William Wilberforce and Thomas Clarkson, the opponents of the slave-trade. There is also a very beautiful sketch of the head of William Wordsworth; this study was made by Pickersgill to save the poet the tedium of long sittings for the portrait in the Hall. It was presented to the College by Miss Arundale, a descendant of the painter. The smaller Combination Room contains many engraved portraits of distinguished members of the College.

The institution of the Combination Room seems gradually to have grown up in colleges as a place where the Fellows might meet together, partly about business, partly for the sake of society. In early times, as the Fellows shared their chambers with their pupils, there could have been no privacy. The room seems to have been called the Parlour for some time; the name Combination Room is now universal at Cambridge, and may have arisen from the fact that the cost of running the room was met by the Fellows combining together for the purpose. At the present time the Combination Room is used for College meetings, as a room where the Fellows meet for a short time after dinner and for dessert on those nights when there is a dinner in Hall to which guests are invited.

The Library.

The Library is only open to visitors by leave of the Librarian, or to those accompanied by a Fellow of the College. The usual access is by staircase E in the Second Court, but leaving the Combination Room by the west door we find ourselves in front of the Library door. The visitor may note that the moulded ceiling of the Combination Room extends overhead. This portion, as we have already seen, originally forming part of the long gallery.

The door of the Library is surmounted by the arms of John Williams, impaled with those of the see of Lincoln. The original position of the Library, as has been already stated, was in the First Court, next the street, and to the south of the entrance gate. In 1616 the books were moved out of this Library to a room over the Kitchen, and in the succeeding year the Master and Fellows wrote to the Countess of Shrewsbury to intimate their intention of building a Library, and hinting at the possibility of her aid in the scheme. The answer of the Countess, if there was one, has not been preserved. In the year 1623, Valentine Carey, Bishop of Exeter, and a former Fellow, wrote announcing that an unnamed person had promised £1200 towards a Library. After some little time Lord Keeper Williams disclosed himself as the donor, and some further advances were promised. The Library was commenced in 1623, and the books finally placed in it in 1628. The style of the building is Jacobean Gothic, and its interior, with the whitewashed walls and dark oak roof and bookcases, is singularly striking. John Evelyn visited it while at Cambridge in 1654, and describes it as "the fairest of that University"; after 250 years the description still holds good.

The upper part of the Library has been little altered since it was built. The intermediate (or lower) cases were heightened to the extent of one shelf for folios when Thomas Baker left his books to the College; but two, one on either hand next the door, retain their original dimensions, with the sloping tops to be used as reading-desks.

At the end of each of the taller cases, in small compartments with doors, are class catalogues written about 1685. These catalogues have been pasted over original catalogues written about 1640; small portions of the earlier catalogues are yet to be seen in some of the cases. Of the treasures in manuscript and print only a slight account can be given here. One of the most interesting to members of the College is the following note by John Couch Adams :—

> "1841 July 3. Formed a design, in the beginning of this week, of investigating, as soon as possible after taking my degree, the irregularities in the motion of Uranus, wh. are yet unaccounted for; in order to find whether they may be attributed to the action of an undiscovered planet beyond it ; and if possible thence to determine the elements of its orbit, &c. approximately, wh. w^d. probably lead to its discovery."

The original memorandum is bound up in a volume containing the mathematical calculations by which Adams carried out his design and discovered the planet Neptune.

Lord Keeper Williams, who was instrumental in building the Library, presented to it many books; amongst others, the Bible known as Cromwell's Bible. Thomas Cromwell employed Miles Coverdale to revise existing translations, and this Bible was printed partly in Paris and partly in London, "and finished in Aprill, A.D. 1539." Two copies were printed on vellum—one for

King Henry VIII., the other for Thomas, Lord Cromwell, his Vicar-General. This College copy is believed to be that presented to Cromwell, and is now unique, the other copy having disappeared from the Royal Library; the volume is beautifully illustrated, and has been described as "the finest book in vellum that exists."

One of the show-cases in the centre contains the service-book which King Charles I. held in his hand at his coronation, and the book used by Laud on the same occasion, with a note in Laud's handwriting: "The daye was verye faire, and ye ceremony was performed wthout any Interruption, and in verye good order." The same case contains the mortuary roll of Amphelissa, Prioress of Lillechurch in Kent, who died in 1299. The nuns of the priory announce her death, commemorate her virtues, and ask the benefit of the prayers of the faithful for her soul. The roll consists of nineteen sheets of parchment stitched together; its length is 39 ft. 3 in., and its average width is about 7 in. There are in all 372 entries of the ecclesiastical houses visited by the roll-bearer for the purpose of gaining prayers for the soul of Amphelissa. The roll-bearer visited nearly all parts of England: there are entries by houses at Bodmin and Launceston in Cornwall; at Dunfermline and St. Andrews in Scotland; each house granting the benefit of its prayers, and concluding in each case with the formula, "*Oravimus pro vestris: orate pro nostris.*" As a collection of contemporary handwritings, such a document has great value; and it is interesting to note that in 600 years the roll has had only two owners, the Priory of Lillechurch and the College, which succeeded to its possession.

In this case there is also an IOU of King Charles II.: "I do acknowledge to have received the summe of one hundred pounds, by the direction of Mr. B., Brusselles the first of April 1660. CHARLES R." The "Mr. B." was John Barwick, a Fellow of the College, afterwards Dean of St. Paul's. The date seems to indicate that the money was advanced to enable Charles to return to England for the Restoration.

In the other show-case there is a very curious Irish Psalter of the eighth century, with crude drawings. Its value is much increased by the fact that the Latin text is interlined throughout with glosses in the Irish dialect.

Of printed books one of the choicest is a very fine Caxton, "The Boke of Tulle of old age; Tullius his book of Friendship." The volume contains the autograph of Thomas Fairfax, the Parliamentary General, who entered the College in 1626. It was presented to the College by Dr. Newcome, Master from 1735 to 1765. To Dr. Newcome the College owes a very fine collection of early printed classics; among these is a copy of Ovid, printed by Jacobus Rubaeus at Venice in 1474; this was formerly in the possession of Lorenzo de Medicis.

Dr. Newcome and Thomas Baker share between them the distinction of having added many of the chief glories of the Library. Matthew Prior, the poet, a Fellow of the College, presented his own works and many interesting French and Italian works on history. There is also a presentation copy from Wordsworth of his poems.

The Kitchen.

The Kitchen (opposite to the Hall) may sometimes be visited when the daily routine permits. The whole has been recently modernised, and a picturesque open fire with rotating spits done away with. To gain more air-space it was necessary to incorporate in the Kitchen some rooms in the floor above. One of these was the set occupied during his College life by the poet Wordsworth, and the fact is commemorated by a stained-glass window.

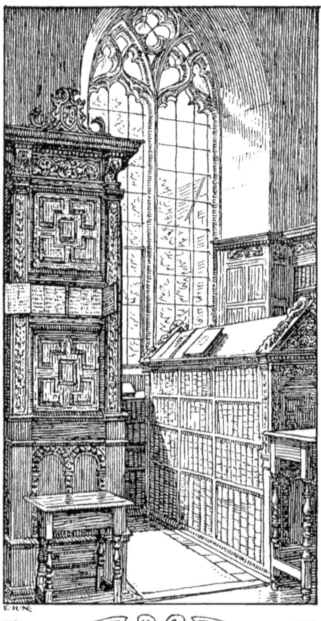

The Library: St John's Coll:

CHAPTER III

THE HOSPITAL OF ST. JOHN

CIRCA 1135–1511

ST. John's College, as we know it, was founded in 1511, and opened in 1516. But at the time of its foundation it took over the buildings and property, and many of the duties, of an earlier and then a venerable foundation, that of the Hospital of St. John the Evangelist in Cambridge. The origin of the old house is obscure, and its earlier history lost, but it seems to have been founded about 1135 by Henry Frost, a burgess of Cambridge. It consisted of a small community of Augustinian canons; its site was described about 140 years later as "a very poor and waste place of the commonalty of Cambridge."

Whatever its early history and endowments may have been, it formed a nucleus for further gifts; and its chartulary, still in the possession of St. John's College, shows a continuous series of benefactions to the old house.

Founded before the University existed, the brethren were occupied with their religious duties, and with the care of the poor and sick who sought their help. An Infir-

35

mary, part of which was adapted for worship, was built. In the thirteenth century a chapel was added, afterwards adapted as the College Chapel, and used as such down to 1869.

Of the domestic buildings practically nothing is known. When some years ago trenches were dug to lay the electric cables for the lighting of the Hall, some traces of a pavement of red tiles were found near the entrance gate of the College.

The Hospital had the opportunity of becoming the earliest College in Cambridge. Hugo de Balsham, Bishop of Ely, obtained in 1280 a licence from King Edward I. to introduce a certain number of scholars of the University into the Hospital, to be governed according to the rules of the scholars of Merton. The regular canons and the scholars were to form one body and one College. The Bishop gave additional endowments to provide for the scholars, but the scheme was a failure. Thomas Baker, the historian of the College, suggests that "the scholars were overwise and the brethren over good." All we do know is that both were eager to part company. The Bishop accordingly removed the scholars in 1284 to his College of Peterhouse, now known as the oldest College in Cambridge. His endowments were transferred with the scholars, and perhaps something besides, for shortly afterwards the brethren complained of their losses. It was then decreed that

Peterhouse should pay twenty shillings annually to the Hospital, an acknowledgment of seniority still made by Peterhouse to St. John's College.

For another two hundred years the Hospital went on, not however forgetting its temporary dignity, and occasionally describing itself, in leases of its property, as the College of St. John.

Towards the end of the fifteenth, or beginning of the sixteenth century, the old house seems to have fallen into bad ways. The brethren were accused of having squandered its belongings, of having granted improvident leases, of having even sold the holy vessels of their Chapel.

At this juncture the Lady Margaret came to the rescue. She had already founded Christ's College in Cambridge, and intended to still further endow the wealthy Abbey of Westminster. Her religious adviser, John Fisher, sometime Master of Michael-House and President of Queens' College in Cambridge, then Bishop of Rochester and Chancellor of the University, persuaded her to bestow further gifts on Cambridge, suggesting the Hospital of St. John as the basis for the new College. The then Bishop of Ely, James Stanley, was her stepson, and in 1507 an agreement was entered into with him for the suppression of the Hospital and the foundation of the College, the Lady Margaret undertaking to obtain the requisite

Bull from the Pope, and the licence of the King. Before this could be carried out King Henry VII. died, 21st April 1509, and the Lady Margaret on the 29th June following.

By her will she had set aside lands to the annual value of £400 for the new College; but innumerable difficulties sprang up. King Henry VIII. was not sympathetic; the Bishop of Ely raised difficulties; the Lady Margaret's own household claimed part of her goods. Fisher has left a quaintly worded and touching memorandum of the difficulties he experienced, but he never despaired. He ultimately got the licence of the King, the requisite Papal Bull, and the consent of the Bishop of Ely. From a letter to Fisher, still preserved in the College, it appears that the " Brethren, late of St. John's House, departed from Cambridge toward Ely the 12th day of March (1510–11) at four of the clokke at afternone, by water."

All facts which have been preserved show Fisher to have been the real moving spirit— to have been the founder in effect, if not in name, and the College from the first has always linked his name with that of the foundress. Of the foundress' estates only one small farm, at Fordham, in Cambridgeshire, came to the College, and that because it was charged with the payment of her debts. What did come was part of what would now be called her personal estate—

moneys she had out on loan, and what could be realised from the sale of her plate and jewels, the furniture and hangings of her various mansions. Rough priced-lists of these, probably handed over by Fisher, are preserved in College.

One personal relic, a manuscript Book of Hours, which belonged to her, was in 1902 presented to the Library by Dr. Alexander Peckover, Lord-Lieutenant of Cambridge-shire.

CHAPTER IV

THE Hospital being closed, the way was cleared for the new College. The Charter, signed by the Executors of the Lady Margaret, is dated 9th April 1511; in this Robert Shorton is named as Master. He held office until on 29th July 1516 the College was opened, when Alan Percy, of the Northumberland House, succeeded. He again was succeeded in 1518 by Nicholas Metcalfe, a member of the Metcalfe family of Nappa Hall, in Wensleydale. Metcalfe had been Archdeacon of Rochester, and was no doubt well known to Fisher as Bishop of that Diocese.

The building of the College commenced under Shorton, but was not finished until about 1520.

It must be remembered that the College was founded before the Reformation, and that these three Masters were priests of the Church of Rome.

Metcalfe was more of an administrator than a student, and his energies were chiefly devoted to the material side of the College interests. Fresh endowments were obtained in place of those which had been lost. King Henry VIII. was persuaded to hand over to the College the estates

THE OLD BRIDGE

of three decayed religious houses — the Maison Dieu at Ospringe, the Nunnery of Lillechurch in Higham, both in Kent, and the Nunnery of Broomhall in Berkshire.

41

As these houses, as well as the Hospital, had allowed their affairs to fall into disorder, it is probable that the identification of their lands, and the reduction of these to effective possession, was a matter of some difficulty. Metcalfe was much absent from College; the accounts of his private expenditure on these journeys have survived, and letters to him from the College during his absences show that his skill and wisdom were much relied on.

Fisher also gave largely to the College, and through his example and influence others were induced to endow fellowships and scholarships. He gave three successive codes of statutes for the government of the College in 1516, 1524, and 1530. These present no novel features, being for the most part based on existing statutes of Colleges at Oxford or Cambridge. They are long, and, as the fashion then was, lay down many rules with regard to minor matters. A few of the leading provisions may be given. One scholar was to be Chapel clerk, to assist the sacrist at Mass; another was to ring the great bell at 4 A.M., as was done before the College was founded, and again at 8 P.M., when the gates were closed; another was to be clock-keeper. These three scholars were to be exempt from all other domestic duties, except that of reading the Bible in time of plague. Seven scholars were told off to serve as waiters in Hall, to bring in and remove the food and dishes ; an eighth was to read the Bible in Hall while the Society were at dinner. When in honour of God, or the Saints, a fire was made up in Hall, the Fellows, scholars, and servants might stay to amuse themselves with singing and repeating poetry and tales. The Master, Fellows, and scholars were to wear clerical dress ; red, white, green, or parti-coloured boots were forbidden.

One-fourth part of the Fellows were always to be engaged in preaching to the people in English ; Bachelors of Divinity, preaching at Paul's Cross, were to be allowed ten days of absence for each sermon. No arms were to be borne, though archery was allowed as a recreation. No Fellow or scholar was allowed to keep hounds, ferrets, hawks, or singing-birds in College. The weekly allowance for commons was 1s. for the Master and each Fellow, 7d. for each scholar. The President or Bursar was to receive a stipend of 40s. a year, a Dean 26s. 8d. No one under the standing of a Doctor of Divinity was to have a separate room ; Fellows and scholars were to sleep singly, or not more than two in a bed. Each room was to have two beds—the higher for the Fellow, the lower or truckle-bed for the scholar ; the truckle-bed being tucked under the other during the day.

The College made an excellent start, and was soon full of earnest and successful students. It is sufficient to mention the names of Sir John Cheke, the famous Greek scholar; of Roger Ascham, the tutor of Queen Elizabeth; and, in another sphere, William Cecil, first Lord Burghley, to give an idea of the influence the College was spreading through her sons.

In all this. Metcalfe had his share. He is the "Good Master of a College" in Fuller's *Holy State*, where we read : "Grant that Metcalfe with Themistocles could not fiddle, yet he could make a little city a great one." And Ascham in *The Scholemaster* writes of him : "His goodnes stood not still in one or two, but flowed aboundantlie over all that Colledge, and brake out also to norishe good wittes in every part of that universitie ; whereby at his departing thence, he left soch a companie of fellowes and scholers in S. Johnes Colledge as can scarce be found now in som whole universitie : which either for divinitie on the one side or other, or for civill service to their Prince and contrie, have bene, and are yet to this day, notable ornaments to this whole Realme. Yea S. Johnes did then so florish, as Trinitie College, that princely house now, at the first erection was but *Colonia deducta* out of S. Johnes, not onelie for their Master, fellowes and scholers, but also, which is more, for their whole both order of learning, and discipline of maners ; and yet to this day it never tooke Master but such as was bred up before in S. Johnes ; doing the dewtie of a

44

good *colonia* to her *metropolis*, as the auncient cities in Greice, and some yet in Italie at this time are accustomed to do."

But troubles were in store both for Fisher and Metcalfe. The Reformation, the divorce of Henry VIII. from Queen Catherine, the Act of Succession, and the sovereign's views on the royal supremacy, were the stumbling-blocks. Fisher went to the Tower, and on 22nd June 1535, to the scaffold ; Metcalfe was compelled to resign in 1537.

Fisher had by deed of gift presented his library to the College, but retained its use for his lifetime—the greatest loan of books on record, as has been said. This magnificent collection was now lost, a loss more lamentable than that of the foundress' estates. Endowments might be replaced, but "the notablest library of bookes in all England" was gone for ever. It is to the credit of the Fellows of the College that, no doubt at some risk to themselves, they stood by Fisher. They visited him in his prison, and in a nobly worded letter stated that as they owed everything to his bounty, so they offered themselves and all they were masters of to his service.

In 1545 King Henry VIII. gave new statutes to the College, adapted to the reformed religion ; but all mention of Fisher and his endowments is cut out ; the College even had to pay 3d. for removing his armorial bearings from the Chapel.

During the reign of King Edward VI.

the outspoken and eloquent Thomas Leaver was Master; on the accession of Queen Mary he, with many of the Fellows, had to fly to Switzerland. In Ascham's words : "mo perfite scholers were dispersed from thence in one moneth, than many years can reare up againe."

The reign of Queen Mary did not extend over much more than five years, but while it lasted a resolute and unflinching effort was made to re-establish the Roman Catholic faith.

The accession of Queen Elizabeth resulted in an equally rapid and fundamental revolution of opinion on the most vital points which can interest mankind. A few selected extracts from the College Account Books for this period bring before us, with almost dramatic effect, the changes which occurred. (Queen Mary succeeded in 1553, Queen Elizabeth on 17th November 1558.)

"1555, To the joyner for setting up the rood, 2*d.*; A new graell printed in parchment 40*s.*;—1556, In Spanish money given to the goldsmyth by Mr Willan to make a pixe to the highe Aultar, 24*s.* 11*d.*; A redde purple velvet cope, with the border of imagrie, having the assumption of our Ladie behinde and three little angels about her and the greater being full of floure de luces, 46*s.* 8*d.*;—1557, To William Allom for two antiphoners, one masse book and hymnal and processioners £6 13*s.* 4*d.*"

THE FIRST CENTURY

"1558, To John Waller and his man for a dayes working pulling down the hye Altar and carrying it away 20*d*.; For pulling down the aulter in Mr Ashton's Chapel 6*d*.; 1563, Received for certain old Albes and other popishe Trashe, sold out of the Revystry the last yere, 26*s*. 10*d*. ; Paid to Mr Baxter for ten Geneva psalters and six service psalters, bought at Christmas last, 22*s*."

This last entry gives us the key to the troubles at St. John's; the Marian exiles had returned with strong Calvinistic leanings. The unrest was, of course, not confined to St. John's, but was general throughout the University. But for the greater part of the reign of Elizabeth there was a strong leaning toward Puritanism in the College. There was a rapid succession of Masters, most of whom were thrust on the College by Court influence ; and about this time the Fellows of St. John's acquired the reputation of being "cunning practitioners" in the art of getting rid of unpopular Masters.

Queen Elizabeth visited Cambridge in August 1564, and was received with all honour. She rode into the Hall of St. John's on her palfrey and listened to a speech from Mr. Humphrey Bohun, one of the Fellows, in which for the last time the restitution of the Lady Margaret's estates was hinted at, without result.

Richard Longworth, a man of Presbyterian sympathies, was at this time Master.

In 1565 he, with the Fellows and scholars, appeared in Chapel without the surplice. Lord Burghley, as Chancellor of the University, wrote a sharply worded letter to Longworth, expressing his grief that such a thing should happen in " my dear College of St. John's " ; adding, " truly no mishap in all my service did ever plunge me more grievously."

Fortunately affairs were in strong and capable hands. With the authority and in the name of Queen Elizabeth, Whitgift, at this time Master of Trinity, afterwards Archbishop of Canterbury, and Cecil provided new statutes for the University in 1570, and for St. John's in 1580. By these much more power was put in the hands of the Master, and government rendered easier to a resolute man.

Matters improved, if not at once, at least gradually, and the Anglican rule became firmly established. But during the mastership of William Whitaker (1586–1595) we still hear of troubles with " Papists." Whitaker was a learned scholar and an acute theologian, but he does not seem to have been a ruler of men or a judge of character. He got involved in an unfortunate dispute with Everard Digby, one of the Fellows, a man of considerable literary reputation, but of a turbulent disposition. Whitaker, who clearly wanted to get rid of Digby, seized upon the pretext that his bill for a month's commons, amounting

to 8s. 7¼d., was left unpaid, and deprived
Digby of his fellowship. An appeal was
lodged with Whitgift and Cecil, who ordered
Whitaker to reinstate Digby. Whitaker
replied that Digby was a Papist, was wont
to blow a horn in the Courts and to holloa
after it, and that he had threatened to put
the President in the stocks ! He seems to
have succeeded in getting rid of Digby for
good.

On the death of Whitaker in 1595,
Richard Clayton became Master. If not
a brilliant scholar, he commanded respect,
and the tenor of many letters which have
come down from that time shows that the
Fellows in residence were on good terms
with each other, and with those of the
Society who had gone out into the world.
The College was prosperous, and the building of the Second Court was the visible
sign of returned efficiency. Clayton lived
on into the reign of King James I., dying
2nd May 1612 ; besides being Master of St.
John's, he was also Dean of Peterborough
and a Prebendary of Lincoln.

During this period the College enjoyed a
considerable reputation as a training ground
for medical men. Thomas Linacre, physician to Henry VIII., founded in 1534 a
medical lectureship in the College, endow-
ing it with some property in London.
The stipend of the lecturer was to be £12
a year, no mean sum in these days—being, in
fact, the same as the statutable stipend of

the Master. In the Elizabethan statutes special and detailed provisions are made for the continuance of the lectureship. These lay down that the lecturer must be versed in the works of Aristotle, and that he should lecture on the works of Galen, which Linacre had translated. The effect of the foundation was to attract a number of medical students to the College, many of whom seem to have obtained fellowships, for we find the Fellows petitioning Queen Elizabeth, while her code of statutes was under consideration, that Divines should be preferred to Physicians in the election of Senior Fellows; otherwise, they submitted, an undue proportion of Physicians would get on the seniority and rule the College. Further, they asked that the medical Fellows, as some return for their privileges, should attend on poor students free of charge. That the College school of medicine was a noted one is confirmed by the fact that three successive Presidents of the Royal College of Physicians were Fellows of St. John's : Richard Smith (1585–1589), William Baronsdale (1589–1600), and William Gilbert (1600–1601). Smith and Gilbert were physicians to Queen Elizabeth ; Baronsdale and Gilbert had been Senior Bursars of the College. Of these Gilbert is the most celebrated ; his treatise, *De Magnete*, is a scientific classic. Galileo spoke of Gilbert as " great to a degree which might be envied." Francis

Bacon mentions the book with applause, and Hallam describes Gilbert as " at once the father of experimental philosophy in this island, and by a singular felicity and acuteness of genius, the founder of theories which have been revived after the lapse of ages, and are almost universally received into the creed of science." Gilbert, who always signs his name Gilberd or Gylberd in the College books, was Senior Bursar of the College in 1569, and President in the succeeding year.

Amongst others who have held the Linacre lectureship, and attained to scientific distinction, was Henry Briggs, who was appointed lecturer in 1592. He afterwards became Gresham Professor of Geometry and Savilian Professor at Oxford. He took up Napier's discovery of logarithms; the idea of tables of logarithims having 10 for their base, and the calculation of the first table of the kind, is due to him.

CHAPTER V

THE SECOND CENTURY
1612–1716

THE second century of the College history opened quietly. Owen Gwyn was elected Master by the choice of the Fellows ; John Williams, then a Fellow, afterwards Lord Keeper, Dean of Westminster, Bishop of Lincoln, and Archbishop of York, exerting himself on Gwyn's behalf. It appears that Williams in after years repented of the choice, and Thomas Baker, the historian of the College, speaks slightingly of Gwyn. Still, under his rule the College flourished, and Williams himself marked the period by providing the greater part of the funds for the new Library.

King James I. and Prince Charles (afterwards Charles I.) frequently visited the University ; James holding his Court at Trinity, but being entertained at St. John's. On one of these occasions, comparing the great Court of Trinity with the two then existing Courts of St. John's, he is said to have remarked that there was no greater difference between the two Societies than between a shilling and two sixpences.

With the advent of the Stuart kings the

HALL, AND CHAPEL TOWER

practice arose of sending mandatory letters
to Colleges, directing the election of named
persons to fellowships. In theory it may
have been correct enough ; the statutes
as enacted by Queen Elizabeth reserved
to herself and her successors the power
of rescinding or altering them. To direct
that the statutory provisions as to elections
should be dispensed with in favour of an
individual was thus within the sovereign's
power, however inconvenient it might prove
in practice. One of the special grievances
at St. John's was that King James directed
the College to elect a Scotchman, George
Seaton, M.A., to a fellowship, though there
was none then actually vacant. The College
obeyed, informing his Majesty that they
had made their statutes wink to fulfil his
bidding, and maintained an extra Fellow for
a time. The practice was, however, fol-
lowed by others ; and Gwyn seems to have
been deluged with letters from persons in
high places, begging for his favour at elections. At some Colleges the device of
" pre-elections " seems to have been resorted
to ; a promising man being elected to the
next fellowship which should be vacant.
Thus, when the vacancy became known,
the College could, with a clear conscience,
say that it had been already filled up ; there
is, however, no trace of this practice at
St. John's.

On Gwyn's death in 1633 there was a
disputed election to the mastership, which

Charles I. settled by nominating William
Beale. Beale was originally a Trinity man,
but had been for about a year Master of
Jesus. He was a supporter of Laud; he em-
bellished the Chapel, and introduced a more
ornate ritual; under his influence St. John's
seems to have been the only College at
Cambridge which fully complied with Laud's
instructions. Thus when the Puritans got
the upper hand, Beale and his College were
the subject of their displeasure.

In 1642 King Charles applied to the
University for supplies. The contribution
of St. John's was £150 in money and 2065
ounces "grocers weight" of silver plate.
The list of the pieces of plate and of the
donors' names is but melancholy reading;
suffice it to say that among those sent were
pieces bearing the names of Thomas Wentworth, Lord Strafford, and of Thomas
Fairfax. The fact that this plate actually
reached the King did not endear the College
to the parliamentary party. Oliver Cromwell surrounded the College, took Dr. Beale
a prisoner, and, to equalise matters, con-
fiscated the communion plate and other
valuables.

Beale, after some imprisonment and wan-
dering, escaped from England and became
chaplain to Lord Cottington and Sir Edward
Hyde (afterwards Lord Clarendon) in their
embassy to Spain; he died at Madrid, and
was there secretly buried. A number of
the Fellows were also ejected, and for some

time the College was used as a prison. The Chapel was stripped of the obnoxious ornaments, and other damage done. A little bundle of papers labelled " Receipts for Army taxes during the Commonwealth " still reposes, as a memento of these days, in the Muniment Room.

St. John's, which dabbled in Presbyterian doctrines during the days of Elizabeth, now had these imposed upon it by superior authority. The two Commonwealth Masters, John Arrowsmith (1644–1653) and Anthony Tuckney (1653–1661), were able men of Puritan austerity, the rule of the latter being the more strict ; judging from the after careers of its members, the College was certainly capably directed. A well-authenticated College tradition relates that when, at an election, the President called upon the Master to have regard to the " godly," Tuckney replied that no one showed greater regard for the truly godly than himself, but that he was determined to choose none but scholars ; adding, with practical wisdom, " They may deceive me in their godliness ; they cannot in their scholarship."

On the Restoration, Dr. Peter Gunning, afterwards Bishop of Ely, was made Master ; and the Earl of Manchester, who, as an officer of the Parliament, was the means of ejecting many of the Fellows, now directed that some of them should be restored to their places. An interesting College custom dates from this period : on the 29th of May in each year the College butler decorates the Hall and Kitchen with fresh oak boughs; there is no order to that effect, but —"it has always been done."

The rest of this century of the College existence, with the exception of one exciting

THE COLLEGE ARMS

event, passed quietly enough. Such troubles as there were in College were but eddies of the storms in the world outside. Of the "seven Bishops" sent to the Tower by King James II. in 1688, three were of St. John's : Francis Turner, Bishop of Ely (who had been Master of the College from 1670 to 1679) ; John Lake, Bishop of

58

Chichester ; and Thomas White, Bishop of Peterborough.

The event of College interest was the fate of the nonjuring Fellows. The Non-jurors were those who, on various grounds, honourable enough, declined to take the oath of allegiance to King William and Queen Mary. Under the law they were liable to be deprived of their places and emoluments. At St. John's twenty Fellows and eight scholars took up the nonjuring position. In the rest of the University there were but fourteen in all, and the same number at the University of Oxford. No explanation seems to be forthcoming as to why there was this preponderance of opinion at St. John's. It is difficult to be-lieve that it was enthusiasm for the cause of James II. ; for when in 1687 that King directed the University to admit Father Alban Francis, a Benedictine monk, to the degree of M.A. without making the sub-scription or taking the oaths required for a degree, Thomas Smoult and John Billers, members of the College (the latter after-wards a Nonjuror), maintained the right of the University to refuse the degree before the notorious Judge Jeffreys, after the Vice-Chancellor and Isaac Newton had been silenced.

Humphrey Gower was at this time Master of the College ; he was of Puritan origin, and entered the College during the Commonwealth. After the Restoration he

joined the Church of England, and though
his sympathies were with the Nonjurors,
he took the oaths and retained his mastership after the flight of King James. He had
been for less than six months Master of
Jesus before becoming Master of St. John's.
Abraham de la Pryme, a member of St.
John's, has handed down an irreverent jest
on his appointment. "Our master, they
say, is a mighty, high, proud man. . . . He
came from Jesus College to be master here,
and he was so sevear that he was commonly
called the divel of Jesus ; and when he was
made master here some unlucky scholars
broke this jest upon him—that now the divel
was entered into the heard of swine ; for us
Johnians are abusively called hoggs."

In 1693 the Court of King's Bench issued
a *mandamus* calling upon Gower to remove
those Fellows who had not taken the oath.
Defence upon the merits of the case there
was none ; but Gower or his legal advisers
opposed the mandate with great skill on
technical points, and after much litigation
the Court had to admit that its procedure
was irregular, and the matter dropped for
some twenty-four years. During this period
some of the Fellows in question died, others
ceded their fellowships owing to the com-
bined action of the general law and the
College statutes. Under the latter Fellows
were bound, when of proper standing, to
proceed to the B.D. degree, but the oath
of allegiance was required of those who took

the degree, and so fellowships were forfeited. Thomas Baker, the historian, who was one of the Nonjurors, had taken the B.D. degree before 1688, so this cause did not operate in his case. But on the accession of King George I., an abjuration oath was required, and the meshes of the net being now smaller, the then Master, Dr. Jenkin, had no other course but to eject Baker and others. The College did all it could to soften the blow, and allowed Baker to reside in College until his death in 1740. He worked unweariedly at his manuscript collections and at the history of the College. The latter was first published in 1869, under the editorship of Professor John E. B. Mayor; with the editor's additions it forms a record of a College such as almost no other foundation can show. Baker's learning and accuracy are undoubted; but it may be permitted (even to a member of his College) to hint that Baker's judgments are a little severe, and his views somewhat narrow.

One notable improvement in the College records dates from this century. In early days no record was made of the names of those who joined the College. The statutes of King Henry VIII. enjoined that a register should be kept of all those admitted to scholarships and fellowships or College offices. This was begun in 1545, and has been continued to the present time. The entries of scholars and Fellows are in the autograph of those admitted, and if they possessed no other interest, have that of providing numerous examples of contemporary handwriting. But of those not admitted on the foundation, or of those admitted prior to 1545, there is no official College record.

Dr. Owen Gwyn and the seniors of his day passed a rule that " the register of the College should have a book provided him wherein he should from time to time write and register the names, parents, county, school, age, and tutor of every one to be admitted to the College." This was commenced in January 1629–30, and has been continued, with varying care and exactness, ever since. It seems probable that the initiative in this matter was due to Gwyn, as few Masters have so carefully preserved their official correspondence.

Just before this general register commenced, three notable men joined the College : Thomas Wentworth, afterwards Earl of Strafford ; Thomas Fairfax, afterwards Lord Fairfax, the victor at Naseby ; and Lucius Cary, Viscount Falkland, who fell in· Newbury fight in September 1643. Complimentary letters to the first and last of these, with the replies, have been preserved. Falkland, in his reply, complains that of the titles given to him by the College " that which I shold most willingly have acknowledged and mought with most justice clayme you were not pleased to vouchsafe me, that of a St. John's man."

Of others who entered we may name : Sir Ingram Hopton, son of Ralph, first Baron Hopton, who entered as a Fellow Commoner 12th May 1631. Sir Ingram fell at the battle of Winceby, 11th October 1643. He there unhorsed Oliver Cromwell in a charge, and knocked him down again as he rose, but was himself killed.

Titus Oates, " the infamous," first entered at Caius 29th June 1667, migrating to St. John's, where he entered 2nd February 1668–69. Thomas Baker for once abandons his decorous reticence and states of Oates : " He was a lyar from the beginning, he stole and cheated his taylor of a gown, which he denied with horrid imprecations, and afterwards at a communion, being admonisht and advised by his Tutor, confest the fact."

Matthew Prior, the poet, was both scholar and Fellow of the College, holding his fellowship until his death. Robert Herrick, though he graduated at Trinity Hall, was sometime a Fellow Commoner here. Thomas Forster of Adderstone, general to the " Old Pretender," and commander of the Jacobite army in 1715, entered the College as a Fellow Commoner 3rd July 1700. Brook Taylor, well known to mathematicians as the discoverer of " Taylor's theorem," entered as a Fellow Commoner 3rd April 1701. While David Mossom of Greenwich, who entered the College as a sizar 5th June 1705, after being ordained, emigrated to America, and became rector of St. Peter's Church, New Kent County, Virginia. He was the officiating clergyman at the marriage of George Washington in St. Peter's Church.

We get an amusing glimpse of the importance of the Master of a College in the following anecdote : " In the year 1712 my old friend, Matthew Prior, who was then Fellow of St. John's, and who not long before had been employed by the Queen as her Plenipotentiary at the Court of France, came to Cambridge ; and the next morning paid a visit to the Master of his own College. The Master (Dr. Jenkin) loved Mr. Prior's principles, had a great opinion of his abilities, and a respect for his character in the world ; but then he had much greater respect for himself. He knew his own dignity too well to suffer a Fellow of his College to sit down in his presence. He kept his seat himself, and let the Queen's Ambassador stand. Such was the temper, not of a Vice-Chancellor, but of a simple Master of a College. I remember, by the way, an extempore epigram of Matt's on the reception he had there met with. We did not reckon in those days that he had a very happy turn for an epigram ; but the occasion was tempting ; and he struck it off as he was walking from St. John's College to the

64

Rose, where we dined together. It was
addressed to the Master :—

> " ' I *stood*, Sir, patient at your feet,
>   Before your elbow chair ;
> But make a bishop's throne your seat,
>   I'll *kneel* before you there.
> One only thing can keep you down,
>   For your great soul too mean ;
> You'd not, to mount a bishop's throne,
>   Pay *homage* to the Queen.' "

CHAPTER VI

THE THIRD CENTURY
1716–1815

THE third century of the College history coincides roughly with the eighteenth century. It was not a period of very high ideals, and " privilege " was in full force. For the first time in the College registers men are entered as " Noblemen." These were allowed to proceed to the M.A. degree direct in two years without passing through the intermediate stage of B.A. The College was also full of Fellow Commoners, who sat with the Fellows at the High Table in Hall ; until the close of the century these do not seem to have proceeded to any degree. The other two classes were the pensioners, who paid their way, and the sizars. A sizar was definitely attached to a Fellow or Fellow Commoner, and in return for duties of a somewhat menial character passed through his College course on reduced terms. Among other duties, a sizar had, with some of the scholars, to wait at table, a service not abolished until 6th May 1786.

Speaking in general terms, the College

THE CHAPEL TOWER FROM THE RIVER.

seems gradually to have acquired the reputation of being the Tory College in the
Whig University ; it became exceedingly
fashionable, and towards the end of the
century had more students in residence
than any other College. At the same time
its reputation for efficiency was very high.
This was due to the policy of Dr. William
Samuel Powell, Master from 1765 to
1775. He introduced various administra-
tive changes on the financial side of College
management, and also started annual examinations in the College, then a novelty
in the University. These examinations
were not very severe, and to the somewhat overtaxed undergraduate of the present
day might seem almost trivial. They were
not competitive, there was no order of
merit, but no one seems to have been
exempt ; their object was simply to test
the knowledge of the students. The suc-
cess of the plan attracted much attention ;
it was proposed to institute similar examinations for the University at large, but
Powell opposed this on the ground that
candidates ought to be examined by those
who taught them. From this date it would
appear that Fellow Commoners, at St.
John's at least, began to take degrees in
the University.

During Powell's mastership an observa-
tory was established on the top of the
western gateway of the Second Court, and
regular astronomical observations taken.

ST. JOHN'S COLLEGE

Two sets of observations there made by
Fellows of the College have been published; one set made by William Ludlam
in 1767 and 1768, the other by Thomas
Catton between 1796 and 1826, the latter
being published by the Royal Astronomical
Society in 1854.

We find members of the College taking
part in all the movements of the time.
In the rebellion of 1745, James Dawson,
a captain in the Manchester Regiment, was
taken prisoner at Carlisle, and executed in
July 1746 on Kennington Common; while
Robert Ganton, afterwards a clergyman,
was excused one term's residence in the
University, during which, as one of "his
majesty's Royal Hunters," he was fighting
the rebels.

Charles Churchill, satirist, was for a short
time a member of the College in 1748.
William Wordsworth, afterwards Poet
Laureate, entered the College as a sizar,
and was admitted a foundress' scholar
6th November 1787. Many adopted
military careers; of these we may mention
George, first Marquis Townshend, who
joined the College in 1741, afterwards
entered the army, and was present at
Fontenoy and Culloden; he went with
Wolfe to Canada, and took over the
command when Wolfe fell. Daniel
Hoghton entered in 1787, he also became
a soldier, and was one of Wellington's
men in the Peninsular War; he was killed

at the battle of Albuera, being then a major-general.

Of another type were William Wilberforce (entered 1776) and Thomas Clarkson (1779), whose names will always be associated in connection with the abolition of slavery. The saintly Henry Martyn, Senior Wrangler in 1801 and Fellow of the College, went out as a missionary to India in 1805, and died at Tokat in Persia in 1812. There have been many missionary sons of the College since his day, but his self-denial greatly impressed his contemporaries, and Sir James Stephen speaks of him as " the one heroic name which adorns the annals of the Church of England from the days of Elizabeth to our own." With Martyn curiously enough is associated in College annals another name, that of Henry John Temple, third Viscount Palmerston, sometime Prime Minister of England ; for Martyn and Temple appear as officers of the College company of volunteers in the year 1803.

Thomas Denman, afterwards Lord Chief Justice, entered the College in 1796 ; he resided in the Second Court, staircase G, at the top. When he brought up his son, the Hon. George Denman, to Trinity he pointed the rooms out to him, and the latter pointed them out to the present writer, " in order that the oral tradition might be preserved."

Alexander John Scott, who, as private

71

secretary and interpreter to Lord Nelson, was present on the *Victory* at Trafalgar, entered the College in 1786, and became a scholar of the College 3rd November 1789. Fletcher Norton, Speaker of the House of Commons from 1770 to 1780, and first Lord Grantley, entered the College in 1734. With him, in a way, was connected John Horne (afterwards Horne Tooke), who entered in 1754 ; for Horne, for purposes of his own, libelled Fletcher Norton when Speaker. Horne Tooke's stormy career belongs rather to political than College history ; but it is worth noting that when he presented himself at Cambridge for the M.A. degree, and the granting of this was opposed in the senate on the ground that he had traduced the clergy in his writings, the members of St. John's, headed by Dr. Richard Beadon, then Public Orator, afterwards Bishop of Bath and Wells, carried the grace for the degree. Horne and Beadon entered the College in the same year.

We have already mentioned Charles Churchill. Another Johnian poet of this period was William Mason, who entered the College in 1742. Mason afterwards became a Fellow of Pembroke, where he was the intimate friend of Thomas Gray. As the biographer of Gray he is perhaps better remembered than for his own poetry, though during his lifetime he enjoyed considerable fame.

A somewhat unusual career was that of William Smith, who entered the College from Eton in 1747, but left without taking a degree. He is reported to have snapped an unloaded pistol at one of the Proctors, and rather than submit to the punishment which the College authorities thought proper to inflict, left the University. He became an actor, and was very popular in his day, being known as "Gentleman Smith." He was associated with David Garrick, and Smith's admirers held that he fell little short of his master in the art.

The reputation of the College as a medical school was maintained by Dr. William Heberden, who entered in 1724. Heberden attended Samuel Johnson in his last illness, and Johnson described him as "*ultimus Romanorum*, the last of our learned physicians." A description which may be amplified by saying that Heberden was in a way the first of the modern physicians.

CHAPTER VII

THE CURRENT CENTURY

THE time has probably not yet come when a satisfactory account of College and University development during the nineteenth century can be written. The changes have been fundamental, involving perhaps a change of ideal as well as of method. In early days the College was filled with men saturated with the spirit of the Renaissance ; casting aside the studies of the Middle Ages, they returned to the literature of Greece and Rome. The ideals of the present day are not less high, but more complex and less easy to state briefly ; the aim is perhaps rather to add to knowledge than to acquire it for its own sake alone.

For the first half of the century College life was still regulated by the statutes of Elizabeth. These were characterised by over-cautious and minute legislation. Now that they are superseded, the chief feeling is one of surprise that a system of laws, intended to be unchangeable, should have endured so long in presence of the changing character of the wants and habits of mankind.

The College
Chapel

It must be remembered that each member of the corporate body, Master, Fellow, or Scholar, on admission, each officer on his appointment, bound himself by oaths of great solemnity to observe these statutes and to seek no dispensation from their provisions. To a more logical race the difficulties must have proved intolerable— the practical Englishman found his own solution.

The forms were observed *juramenti gratia*, but much practical work was supplemental to the statutes. This could be illustrated in more than one way—the most interesting is the development of the educational side and the tutorial system.

The statutes prescribed the appointment of certain lecturers—even the subjects of their lectures. Space need not be occupied in showing that such provisions soon became obsolete. The working solution was found in the tutorial system. In early days it was contemplated and prescribed that each Fellow should have the care of two or three students, living with them, teaching them daily ; the exact date when this system passed away has not been traced with any certainty, but gradually the number of Fellows taking individual charge of the undergraduates diminished until it became reduced to two or three. Those in charge became known as Tutors, and with each Tutor was associated one or two others called Assistant Tutors or Lecturers. A charge was made to the undergraduates for tuition, and the sum so received was shared by the Tutors and their assistants. But the Tutor was not a College officer in the eye of the statutes, nor the money received for tuition treated as part of the College revenues. The system worked, because it was meant to work, and as it was not subject to obsolete rules could be modified and adapted to changing conditions. So long as the chief subjects of study were few in number, practically restricted to classics and mathematics, College provision for teaching was possible and simple. The multiplication of studies, the needs of the studies generally known as the Natural Sciences, with their expensive laboratories and equipment, are entailing further changes, and the tendency, more especially in the newer subjects, is to centralise teaching under the control of University professors and teachers. The subject is one of great interest, but cannot be further touched upon here. To return to the history of St. John's.

Dr. James Wood became Master in 1815. He was a man of humble origin, a native of Holcombe, in the parish of Bury, Lancashire. According to a well-authenticated tradition he "kept," as an undergraduate, in a garret in staircase O in the Second Court, and studied in the evening by the light of the rush candle which lit the staircase, with his feet in straw, not being able to afford fire or light. He became a successful and popular College Tutor, and his mathematical writings were long the standard text-books in the University. At the time of his death in 1839 he held, with his mastership, the Deanery of Ely and the Rectory of Freshwater in the Isle of Wight. He made the College his residuary legatee, but during his life had handed over large sums for College purposes, and the total of his gifts cannot have been less than £60,000.

In Wood's time we find the first movement in favour of change taken by the College itself. St. John's then suffered under a specially awkward restriction arising from the joint effect of the general statutes and the trusts of private foundations. By the statutes not more than two Fellows could come from any one county in England, or more than one from each diocese in Wales.

There were thirty-two foundation Fellows, and twenty-one founded by private benefactors, the latter having all the privileges and advantages of the former. Each of these private foundations had its own special restriction ; the holders were to be perhaps of founder's name or kin, or to come from certain specified counties, parishes, or schools. The effect of these special restrictions was that many fellowships had to be filled by men possessing the special qualification without, perhaps, any great intellectual distinction. But once a county was "full" no

Fellow could be elected who had been born in that county; and even if a vacancy occurred a promising man might be again cut out by some special restriction. Dr. Wood and the Fellows addressed themselves to this point and obtained in 1820 the Royal consent to a statute throwing open the foundress' fellowships without restriction as to county; the private foundations were left untouched, but the College was empowered to transfer a Fellow on the foundress' foundation to one of the special foundations, if qualified.

Dr. Wood was succeeded as Master by Dr. Ralph Tatham, whose father and grandfather (of the same names) had been members of the College. He was Public Orator of the University from 1809 to 1836, an office for which he was well qualified by a singular dignity of person and courtesy of manner. "He brought forth butter," said the wags, "in a lordly dish." In the year 1837 the Earl of Radnor and others raised the question of University reform, and tried to induce the House of Lords to pass a bill for the appointment of a University Commission. In the end the matter was shelved, the friends of the University undertaking that the Colleges, with the approval of their Visitors, should prepare new statutes for the assent of the Crown. The change in St. John's was opposed by some ultra-conservative Fellows, who urged that as they were bound by oath to observe and uphold the statutes, and to seek no dispensation from them, they were precluded from asking for any change. The Bishop of Ely, however, gently put this objection on one side, and the statutes then prepared were approved by Queen Victoria in 1849. The more ardent reformers have described this code as merely legalising the customs and "abuses" which had grown up around the Elizabethan statutes without introducing any effective change.

On the death of Dr. Tatham (19th January 1857), Dr. William Henry Bateson was elected Master ; he had been Senior Bursar of the College from 1846, and Public Orator of the University from 1848. Dr. Bateson was a man of scholarly tastes, but he was above all a practical man of affairs and of broad views. He served on more than one University Commission appointed to examine into and report upon the University and Colleges. The College statutes were twice revised during his mastership; the first code becoming law in 1860, the second was prepared during his lifetime, though it did not become law till a year after his death. These statutes are much less interesting reading than the early statutes, though undoubtedly more useful. While aiming at precision in the matter of rights and duties, they leave great freedom in matters of study, discipline, and administration. All local restrictions on scholarships and fellowships have been abolished. The government of the College is entrusted to a Council of twelve, elected by the Fellows, and presided over by the Master; a simple method has been provided of altering them if necessary. Independently of the changes thus introduced the College, on its own initiative, was providing for the newer studies. In 1853 a chemical laboratory was built, and a lecturer in chemistry appointed, and other lecturers appointed from time to time as the scope of University teaching was widened. St. John's at an early date began to elect men to scholarships and fellowships for Natural Science. In all this we may trace the influence of Dr. Bateson, one of whose guiding principles was to widen and increase the teaching power of the College, and to reward intellectual distinction of any kind. Dr. Bateson died 27th March 1881, and was succeeded by Dr. Charles Taylor, the present Master.

Of men who have added lustre to the College roll of worthies we may mention Sir John F. W. Herschel, the astronomer, who was Senior Wrangler in 1813, and died in 1871, laden with all the honours which scientific and learned bodies could bestow upon him; he lies buried in Westminster Abbey close to the tomb of Newton. John Couch Adams, Senior Wrangler in 1843, in July 1841, while yet an undergraduate, resolved to investigate the irregularities in the motion of the planet Uranus, with the view of determining whether they might be attributed to an undiscovered planet. The memorandum he made of his resolve is, as has been stated, now in the College Library. It is a matter of history how Adams carried out his purpose, and how through a series of unlucky accidents he did not get the sole credit for his discovery of the planet Neptune. Adams became a Fellow of the College in 1843, but had to vacate his fellowship in 1852 as he was not in orders. The College tried to induce a Mr. Blakeney, who then held one of the very few fellowships tenable by a layman, to resign his fellowship and make way for Adams; offering to pay him for the rest of his life an income equal to that of his fellowship. Mr. Blakeney, however, refused, and a fellowship was found for Mr. Adams at Pembroke College, which he held till his death.

It is perhaps a delicate matter to allude to those still living, but two may perhaps be mentioned. The Hon. Charles A. Parsons by his development of the steam turbine has revolutionised certain departments of engineering. Dairoku Kikuchi, the first Japanese student to come to Cambridge, after graduating in 1877, in the same year as Mr. Parsons, returned to Japan, and has held many offices, including that of Minister of Education, in his native country.

We may say that the changes introduced in the nineteenth century have restored to the College its national character, admitting to the full privileges of a University career certain classes of students who had been gradually excluded. During the reigns of Henry VIII., Edward VI., Mary, and Elizabeth, there was always a part of the nation, Protestant or Roman Catholic, which found the entry barred to it. The establishment of the Anglican rule in the reign of Elizabeth led to the exclusion of Roman Catholics, and for three hundred years the doors of the University were closed to them.

The Civil Wars, the Commonwealth, and the Restoration produced religious difficulties of another kind; the wholesale ejections in 1644 and 1660 testify to the troubles men had to face for conscience' sake. After the Restoration the Puritan, the Protestant Dissenter, was excluded with the Romanist.

In the eighteenth century a certain variety was introduced by the entry of students from the West Indies, sons of planters; one or two individuals came from the American colonies. The constant wars drew off men to military careers, and the religious movements towards the close of the century attracted men, after leaving College, to Unitarianism or Wesleyanism. The celebrated Rowland Hill was a member of the College; Francis Okeley, after leaving, became a Moravian or a Mystic. Such dissenters as entered the College, and they were very few, were obliged to leave without graduating.

The removal of all religious tests has

thus restored to the ancient Universities a national character they had not possessed since the early days of Henry VIII., when all could come, as all were practically of the same faith.

Thus a wider field is open to the College to draw on, not only in the British Islands, but in all its colonies and dependencies. On the other hand, it is no less true that her sons are to be found more widely scattered. A hundred and fifty years ago one could say of a selected group of men that the majority would become clergymen or schoolmasters, a few would become barristers, others would return to their country estates, one or two might enter the army; with that we should have exhausted the probabilities. Now there is probably not a career open to educated men in which members of the College are not to be found; the State in every department, civil, ecclesiastical, or military, enlists her sons in its service. The rise of scientific industries has opened new careers to trained men. We talk of the spacious days of Elizabeth; if space itself has not increased it is at least more permeated with men who owe their early training to the foundation of the Lady Margaret.

CHAPTER VIII

SOCIAL LIFE

HITHERTO we have confined ourselves to an outline of the College
history on what may be called its official
side. In what follows we deal briefly with
some features of the life of the place.

The original, and perhaps the chief,
purpose of the College in the eyes of those
who founded it was practically that it should
form a training ground for the clergy. The
statutes of King Henry VIII. distinctly lay
down that theology is the goal to which
philosophy and all other studies lead, and
that none were to be elected Fellows who
did not propose to study theology. The
statutes of Elizabeth provided a certain
elasticity by prescribing that those Fellows
who did not enter priests' orders within six
years should vacate their fellowships; but
that two Fellows might be allowed, by the
Master and a majority of the Senior Fellows,
to devote themselves to the study of medicine. King Charles I. in 1635 allowed a
like privilege to be granted from thenceforth
to two Fellows who were to study law.
These privileges were not always popular,
and we occasionally find the clerical Fellows

THE NEW COURT

complaining that while the duties of teaching and catechising were laid on them, a man who had held one of the law or medical fellowships sometimes took orders late in life and then claimed presentation to a College benefice in virtue of his seniority as a Fellow, having in the meantime escaped the drudgery to which the Fellow in orders had been subject.

The emoluments of members of the Society in early times were very modest, and as prices rose became quite inadequate ; the amounts being named in the College statutes were incapable of alteration, and indirect means were taken to provide relief. In Bishop Fisher's time it was considered that an endowment of £6 a year sufficed to found a fellowship, and £3 a year to found a scholarship. The statutable stipend of the Master was only £12 a year, though he had some other allowances, the total amount of which was equally trivial. James Pilkington, Master from 1559 to 1561, when he became Bishop of Durham, wrote to Lord Burghley on the subject of his successor, stating that whoever became Master must have some benefice besides to enable him to live. Richard Longworth, Master from 1564 to 1569, made a similar complaint, putting the weekly expenses of his office at £3. We accordingly find that many of the Masters held country benefices, prebends, or deaneries with their College office. Lord Keeper Williams, who gave

to the College the advowsons of Soulderne
in Oxfordshire, Freshwater in the Isle of
Wight, and the sinecure rectories of St.
Florence and Aberdaron in Wales, made it
part of the conditions of his gift that the
Master should always be entitled to take
one of these livings if a vacancy occurred.
Many of the Fellows also held benefices or
curacies near Cambridge. In the eighteenth
century the business of holding ecclesiastical
preferment in plurality became almost a fine
art; thus Sir Isaac Pennington, who was
President of the College and Regius Professor of Physic, left to the College by his
will a fund to provide the sum of £200 a
year for the Master "if he be rector of
Freshwater and not otherwise," a direct
and curious incentive to holding in plurality.
A Fellow was entitled to his commons, and,
in addition, to allowances of 13s. 4d. under
each of the three heads of "corn," "livery,"
and "stipend," or, as we may say, food,
clothes, and pocket-money. The College
officers received but small salaries, the most
highly paid being the President and Senior
Bursar, who each received £2.

An effort was made by the Statutes of the
Realm to improve the condition of members
of colleges. It seems to have been assumed
that the rent of a college farm, like its
statutes, could not be altered; but by an Act
of Parliament passed in the eighteenth year
of Elizabeth, known as Sir Thomas Smith's
Act, it was enacted that from thenceforth

one-third of the rents were to be paid in
wheat and malt ; the price of wheat for
the purposes of the Act being assumed to be
6s. 8d. a quarter, and of malt 5s. a quarter.
Thus if before the Act the rent of a farm
was £6 a year, after it became law the
tenant had to pay £4 in money, three-
quarters of wheat, and four quarters of malt,
these two latter items coming to £1 each.
But the tenant now paid a rent varying
according to the prices of the day—namely,
the money rent plus the cash value of the
wheat and malt according to the best prices
of these commodities in Cambridge on the
market-day preceding quarter-day. Thus
as the prices of wheat and malt rose the
College benefited. By the Act this variable
one-third, or "corn-money," went to increase the allowance for commons. As
time went on the amount of the corn-
money was more than sufficient to pay for
the commons, and a further modest allowance out of the surplus was made to all who
participated in the College revenues, whether
as Master, Fellow, scholar, or sizar, under
the name of *præter*.

In process of time another source of
revenue arose. Leases of College estates
were usually granted for a term of forty
years, and there was a general custom that
the tenant might surrender his lease at the
end of fourteen years and receive a new
one for forty years. As prices rose tenants
were willing to pay a consideration for the

renewal known as a "fine"—this was calculated on the full letting value of the estate at the time of the renewal, the rent reserved remaining at its traditional amount. At first this fine-money was regarded as a species of surplus, and grants were made from it to Fellows or scholars who were ill or in special need of temporary assistance. The cost of entertaining royalties or other distinguished visitors, and part of the cost of new buildings, were defrayed from this source. In the year 1629 the practice arose of dividing this fine-money up among the Master and Fellows in certain shares, and the money so paid became known as the "dividend." At the present time the College property is managed like any other landed estate, and after the necessary expenses of management and maintenance have been met, and certain fixed sums paid to the scholars and exhibitioners, and to the University, the remainder is by the statutes divided up into shares called dividends, each Fellow getting one dividend, the Master and the members of the College Council receiving certain additions calculated in dividends; there is a general restriction that the dividend shall not exceed £250 a year. The fall in the value of land at present automatically provides that this limit is not exceeded; if the revenues become more than sufficient for the purpose, additional fellowships and scholarships must be established.

The reader will gather that the chief

endowment of the College arises from land. The College estates lie scattered over most of the eastern side of England, from Yorkshire to Kent. There is no large block of property anywhere. The estates in past times, when means of communication were poor, must have been difficult to visit. In the leases of the more distant farms it was usual to stipulate that the tenant should provide "horse meat and man's meat" for the Master and Bursar and their servants while on a tour of inspection. That some care was bestowed on the management is clear from the regular entries, in the books of accounts, of the expenses of those "riding on College business." Probably the estates were visited when leases came to be renewed, and an effort made to discover the actual letting value of the property. Land agents seem to have been first employed to make formal valuations towards the end of the eighteenth century, and about the same time plans of the estates were obtained, some of these, made before the enclosures, showing the land scattered in many minute pieces, are very curious and interesting.

The actual life within the College walls is not so easy to describe with any certainty. At first, as we have seen, the undergraduates actually lived with Fellows of the College, and overcrowding must have been a constant feature of College life. On 15th December 1565 a return was made to Lord Burghley of all students, "whether tutors or pupils," residing in the College, with notes as to whether they had come into Chapel in their surplices or not. The return concludes with this summary : " The whole number is 287, whereof there came into the Chappell with surplesses upon the last Saturdaie and Sondaie 147 ; and abrode in the country 33. And of thother 107 whiche cumme not in as yet, there be many cumme to the Colledge of late and be not yet provided of surplesses." At this time we have to remember that the buildings of the College consisted only of the First Court, the Infirmary or Labyrinth, and a small block of buildings in a corner of the ground now occupied by the Second Court, swept away when that was built. The arrangement seems to have been as follows. The ground-floor rooms were occupied by junior Fellows, each with a few pupils. The rooms on the first floor, known in the College books as the " middle chambers," were in greater request ; with these went the rooms on the second floor, with sometimes *excelses,* or garrets over them —these could accommodate a senior Fellow with several pupils. In the older parts of the College the rooms occupied the whole depth of the building, and so were lighted from both sides ; in the corners, when light could be obtained, cubicles or studies were partitioned off. From a sanitary point of view, life under such conditions must have left much to be desired, and the burial registers of All Saints' parish (in which the

older part of the College is situated) leave
the impression of frequent and almost epi-
demic illness in the College during the
sixteenth and early part of the seventeenth
century.

The undergraduates in early times were
much younger than the men of the present
day. The statutes prescribed that the oath
should not be required from scholars who
were under sixteen years of age; the frequent
occurrence of *non juratus* in the admission
entry of a scholar shows that many came
to the College before that age. Probably
the average age was about sixteen ; the idea
being that after the seven years' residence
required for the M.A. degree they would
be of the proper age to present themselves
for ordination. Those under eighteen years
of age might be publicly whipped in the
Hall for breaches of discipline.

Students from distant parts of England
probably resided continuously in College
from the time they entered it until they
took their degrees. The statutes of King
Henry VIII. contemplate a period of some
relaxation at Christmas ; providing that
each Fellow in turn should be " Lord " at
Christmas, and prepare dialogues and plays
to be acted by members of the College
between Epiphany and Lent. The brazier
in the Hall seems to have been kept burning
in the evening about Christmas time ; of
this practice a curious relic survived until
comparatively lately, it being the custom to

leave a few gas-jets burning in the Hall until midnight from St. John's Day (December 27) until Twelfth Night.

There were three classes of students. The Fellow Commoners, sons of noblemen or wealthy land-owners, who sat at the High Table, or, as it was phrased, were in Fellows' commons. Some came in considerable state. In 1624 the Earl of Arundel and Surrey sent his two sons, Lord Maltravers and Mr. William Howard, to the College. The Earl's chaplain, or secretary, in making arrangements for their coming, wrote to request that they should have one chamber in the College, with a "pallett for the gromes of their chamber"; the rest of "his lordships company, being two gentlemen, a grome of his stable and a footman, may be lodged in the towne near the College." At this period the Second Court had been built, and the accommodation for residence thus somewhat. greater than in Elizabethan times. The Fellow Commoner wore a gown ornamented with gold lace, and a cap with a gold tassel. The last Fellow Commoner at St. John's to wear this dress was the present Admiral Sir Wilmot Hawksworth Fawkes.

The next class in order of status were the Pensioners—men who paid their expenses without assistance from the College, sons of middle-class parents. In times of which we have any definite record this was the most numerous class in College. Lastly, we have the sizars. A sizar was definitely attached to a Fellow or Fellow Commoner; he was not exactly a servant, but made himself generally useful. For example, those members of the College who absented themselves from the University sermon were in the eighteenth century fined sixpence, and the sizars were expected to mark the absentees. The sizar at Cambridge had, however, always a better status than the servitor at Oxford, and in the days when scholarships were strictly limited as to locality, a sizarship was something of the nature of what at the present day we should describe as an entrance scholarship or exhibition, the assistance given consisting in a reduction of expenses rather than in actual direct emolument. At the present time there is no difference in status among members of the College; the foundation scholars, however, having special seats in Chapel and a separate table in Hall if they choose to make use of it.

Until 1882 the condition of celibacy attached to all fellowships in the College; Queen Elizabeth held strong views on the matter, even discouraging the marriage of Masters. The necessity of taking orders was somewhat relaxed in 1860. The system had its advantages—it tended to produce promotion; for the natural inclination of mankind to marry, vacated fellowships; the disadvantage was that men with a real taste for study or teaching had no certain career before them. The question of allowing Fellows to marry was raised in the eighteenth century, but met with little support and much opposition. Even in

THE "BRIDGE OF SIGHS"

the middle of the nineteenth century a University Commission inclined to the view that celibacy was inseparable from the collegiate system.

The clerical restriction had the effect of chiefly confining selection to College offices to those who were in orders. These in due course went off to benefices in the gift of the College, these acting as a species of pension. One form of benefaction frequently bestowed by past members was the gift of an advowson ; one or two benefactors left estates, the revenues from which were to accumulate, and with the sums so raised advowsons were to be purchased. Presentation to livings went by seniority of standing, and this practice, with the restriction on marriage, gave rise to the belief, still prevalent in many parishes where the College is patron, that the College on a vacancy always chooses for the next incumbent "the oldest bachelor." It seems probable, without any minute statistical inquiry, that most of the Fellows left the College before the age of forty. A few remained on for life.

It is difficult now to reconstruct a picture of the High Table, made up as it was for many years of a group of middle-aged or elderly men, with a considerable admixture of youthful Fellow Commoners. During the eighteenth century the proportion of Fellow Commoners was probably from one-fourth to one-third of those dining together, and constraint on both sides must have been almost inevitable. The terms "don" and "donnishness" seem to have acquired their uncomplimentary meaning about this period. The precise significance of "don" is not easy to express concisely ; the most felicitous is perhaps that of the Oxford *Shotover Papers*, where we read that don means, in Spain, a gentleman ; in England, a Fellow. The abolition of the Fellow Commoner was perhaps chiefly due to the rise of the democratic spirit and a general dislike of privilege, but there are other grounds for welcoming it.

Of the individuals who make up the stream of youthful life which has ebbed and flowed through the College gate there is but little official record. An Admonition Book exists, in which more than a century ago those who were punished for graver offences against discipline signed the record of their sentence and promised amendment. One youth admits over a trembling signature that he was "admonished by the Master, before the Seniors, for keeping strangers in my chamber till twelve o' the clock, and disturbing the Master by knocking at his gate in an irreverent manner at that hour for the keys of the gate." When the College gate was closed it may be explained that the keys were placed in the Master's keeping. We are, however, left in ignorance of what passed in that chamber until the midnight hour. Yet no doubt the student in past days had his amusements as well as his successor of the present day—rougher perhaps, but not less agreeable to him.

In Bishop Fisher's statutes archery was encouraged as a pastime, and we know from Ascham's writings that he indulged in it. In the sixteenth century the College built a tennis-court for the use of its members. John Hall, who entered the College in 1646, recommended " shittlecock " as fit for students—" it requires a nimble arme with quick and waking eye." We hear of horse matches and cock-fighting, but in terms of disapproval. Football is mentioned in 1574, when the Vice-Chancellor directed that scholars should only play upon their own College ground. In 1595 " the hurtful and unscholarly exercise of football " was forbidden, except within each College and between members of the same College. Certain general orders for the discipline of the undergraduates, which gave rise to much controversy about 1750, forbade cricket between the hours of nine and twelve in the morning. In 1763 the Vice-Chancellor required that no scholar, of whatever rank, should be present at bull-baiting. We read in the eighteenth century of " schemes " or water-parties on the river, but these appear to have been more of the nature of picnics than exercises of skill. Riding was probably very common, the student arriving on his nag, perhaps selling it and using the proceeds as a start in his new life. The phrase " Hobson's choice " took its rise from the rule in the livery stables of Hobson the carrier that a man who hired a hack had to take the one that stood nearest to the stable door. In later days stage - coaches supplied a more regular means of conveyance.

Students leaving Cambridge for the North betook themselves to Huntingdon, and were housed at the George Inn there till places could be found for them in the coaches. The landlord of the George sending over to Cambridge to let it be known that one batch were gone and that another might come over.

Traditions linger in parishes round Cambridge that the University "gentlemen" used certain fields or commons for the purpose of riding races ; the Cottenham steeplechases are presumably a survival of this practice. Shooting and coursing, with a little hunting, came into vogue at the end of the eighteenth century.

The rise and organisation of athletic sports as an essential element of College life would require a bulky history in itself. The first to take definite form was rowing. The historic boat club of the college is the Lady Margaret Boat Club ; this was founded in the October term of 1825. The actual founder of the club seems to have been the Hon. Richard John Le Poer Trench, a son of the second Earl of Clancarty. Trench afterwards became a captain in the 52nd Regiment, and died 12th August 1841. The club was the first to start an eight-oared boat on the Cam, though some Trinity men had a four-oar on the river a short time before the Lady Margaret was started. Among the first members of the club were William Snow and Charles Merivale, afterwards Dean of Ely. Trench acted as stroke of the original first boat crew in the Lent Term of 1826. There were at first no regular races, but impromptu trials of speed with other crews frequently took place. In 1827 the University Boat Club was started, and regular bumping races begun. The first challenge to Oxford was determined on at a meeting of the University Boat Club held 20th February 1829, when it was resolved : " That Mr. Snow, of St. John's, be requested to write immediately to Mr. Staniforth, Christ Church, Oxford, proposing to make up a University Match." The match was made up, and the race rowed at Henley on 10th June 1829, and from this the annual boat-race between Oxford and Cambridge takes its rise. Snow acted as stroke of the Cambridge boat, George Augustus Selwyn, successively Bishop of New Zealand and Lichfield, rowed " seven," and Charles Merivale " four." Snow (afterwards Strahan) became a banker, and died at Florence 4th July 1886. In after years when, from 1861 to 1869 inclusive, Oxford had uniformly beaten Cambridge, the Lady Margaret supplied the late John H. D. Goldie to break the spell and restore hope and confidence to Cambridge crews. Thus the College club has taken an important part in the establishment and maintenance of Cambridge rowing. Two verses of the College boat song run as follows :—

" Mater regum Margareta
    Piscatori dixit laeta
        ' Audi quod propositum ;
    Est remigium decorum
    Suavis strepitus remorum
        Ergo sit Collegium.'

.   .   .   .   .

    Sic Collegium fundatum
    Et Johannis nomen datum
        Margareta domina,
    Ergo remiges gaudendum
    Triumphandum et canendum
        In saeclorum secula."

So that, if we can trust the historic in-
sight of the author (Mr. T. R. Glover), the
intentions of the foundress have been duly
carried out.

The uniform of the club was at first
much what it is now, a white jersey with
pink stripes; with this was worn a jacket
of scarlet flannel, popularly known as a
" blazer "—a name which has passed into
the English language as descriptive of the
coloured jackets of all clubs. It is said that
some one, whose feeling for analogy was
stronger than for decorum, described the
surplice as "the blazer of the Church
of England." Organised cricket clubs,
athletic clubs, and football clubs grew up,
and in process of time clubs for the pursuit
of every kind of athletic exercise have been
started. Originally each club in College
had a subscription, paid by its members,
towards the expenses of the special game.
About twenty years ago all the clubs in
St. John's were united into one club—

"The Amalgamation." The subscription to this entitles a member to join in any of the recognised games. The funds are administered by a committee consisting of the representatives of those interested in the different games, and grants made from the general fund towards the expenses of each game. The presence of a few senior members of the College on the committee provides the continuity so difficult to maintain with the short-lived generations of undergraduate life. The College provides the ground for the cricket, football, and lawn-tennis clubs, while through the generosity of members of the College of all standings a handsome boat-house has recently been built on the river. The College also possesses flourishing musical and debating societies, and from time to time clubs arise for literary and social purposes, dying out and being refounded with great persistence.

In another sphere of work the College has taken a leading part. St. John's was the first College in Cambridge to start a mission in London—the Lady Margaret Mission in Walworth. Preaching in the College Chapel on 28th January 1883, the Rev. William Allen Whitworth, a Fellow of the College, then Vicar of St. John's, Hammersmith, afterwards Incumbent of All Saints', Margaret Street, suggested that the College should support a mission in some neglected district of London. The matter took form a little later in the year, and since then the College Mission has been a College institution. Members of the College visiting the mission district, and visitors from Walworth coming for an annual outing, including a cricket match, in August.

Another flourishing institution is the College magazine, *The Eagle*. Founded in the year 1858, it has maintained its existence for nearly fifty years, being now the oldest of College magazines. It has numbered among its contributors many who have subsequently found a wider field and audience : some of the earliest efforts of Samuel Butler, author of *Erewhon*, are to be found in its pages.

I now bring my sketch of the College history to a close. I have endeavoured, within the prescribed limits, to give an outline of the corporate life of an ancient and famous foundation. In writing it two classes of readers have been borne in mind : the visitor who, within a short compass, may wish to learn something more than can be picked up by an inspection of the buildings ; members of the College who feel a lively interest in the habits and pursuits of those who have preceded them. I have, perhaps, thought more of the latter than of the former class.

Members of the College have always been distinguished for a certain independence of thought and adherence to principle,

not always guided by motives of mere
worldly prudence; they have always been
noted for that strong corporate feeling
which finds expression in the words of
Viscount Falkland's letter, before alluded
to : "I still carry about with me an indel-
ible character of affection and duty to that
Society, and an extraordinary longing for
some occasion of expressing that affection
and that duty."

To one who has spent much of his life
in the service of the institution to which
he owes so much, the words of the Psalmist
(a Scot naturally quotes the version en-
deared to him by early association) seem
to put the matter concisely—

> " For in her rubbish and her stones
> thy servants pleasure take ;
> Yea, they the very dust thereof
> do favour for her sake."

INDEX

ADAMS, J. C., 16, 25, 26, 29, 82
Admonition Book, 100
Armorial Bearings, 2
Arrowsmith, J., 57
Ascham, R., 19, 23, 44
Ashton, H., 19

BAKER, T., 28, 32, 61
Balsham, Hugo de, 36
Baronsdale, W., 50
Barwick, J., 31
Bateson, W. H., 81
Beale, W., 56
" Blazer," 104
Blunt, J. J., 22
Boat Club, 102
Bohun, H., 47
" Bridge of Sighs," 8, 10
Briggs, H., 51
Brown, " Capability," 10
Bull-baiting, 101
Burghley, Lord, 18, 48

CAREY, V., 28
Catton, T., 70
Caxton, 31
Celibacy, 97
Chapel, New, 13-17
Chapel, Old, 4, 13
Charles I., 26, 30, 52, 56, 86
Charles II., 31
Cheke, Sir J., 44
Churchill, C., 70, 72
Clarkson, T., 26
Clayton, R., 49
Clive, R. H., 22
College Leases, 91
Combination Room, 5, 23, 25, 27

Commons, 43, 90
Corn Rents, 91
Cricket, 101
Cromwell, O., 56, 63
Cromwell, T., 29, 30

DALLAM, R., 22
Dawson, J., 70
Denman, T., 71
Digby, E., 48
Dividend, 92

Eagle, The, 106
Eagle Close, 10
Edward VI., 45
Elizabeth, Queen, 46, 47
Estates, 93
Examinations, 24, 69

FAIRFAX, T., 31, 56, 62
Falkland, Viscount, 18, 62, 107
Fawkes, Sir W. H., 96
Fellow Commoners, 66, 96, 97, 99
Fisher, John, 37
Floods, 7
Football, 101
Forster, T., 63
Frost, H., 35

GANTON, R., 70
Gilbert, W., 18, 50, 51
Glover, T. R., 104
Goldie, J. H. D., 103
Gower, H., 7, 59, 60
Gunning, P., 57
Gwyn, O., 52, 62

INDEX

HALL, THE, 23
Hare, Sir R., 25
Hawksmoor, N., 8
Heberden, W., 73
Henrietta Maria, Queen, 26
Henry VII., 38
Henry VIII., 18, 38, 41, 45, 86
Herrick, R., 63
Herschel, Sir J. F. W., 25, 26, 82
High Altar, 46
Hill, R., 84
Hoare, H., 16
Hoghton, General, 70
Hopton, Sir I., 63
Horne Tooke, 72
Hospital of St. John, 14, 35
Howard, Lord Thomas, 3
Hutchinson, H., 8

INFIRMARY, 17

JAMES I., 26, 49, 52
James II., 58
Jenkin, R., 61, 64

KENNEDY, B. H., 25
Kikuchi, D., 83
Kirke White, H., 4, 20
Kitchen, 32
Knox, E., 17
Knox, John, 17
Knox, N., 17

LABYRINTH, 17, 18, 94
Lady Margaret, 1, 2, 37
Laud, 30
Leases, 92
Library, 25, 27, 28
Lillechurch, 30, 41
Linacre, T., 49
Liveing, G. D., 25
Longworth, R., 47, 89
Ludlam, W., 70

MARTYN, H., 71
Mary, Queen, 46
Mason, W., 72
Master's Lodge, 15, 25

Mayor, J. E. B., 25, 61
Mengs, R. A., 22
Merivale, C., 102, 103
Metcalfe, N., 20, 40, 42
Mission, Walworth, 105
Mortuary Roll, 30
Mossom, D., 63

NEWCOME, J., 31
Nonjurors, 59
Norton, F., 72

OATES, Titus, 63
Okeley, F., 84
Organ, 22
Ospringe, 41

PALMER, E. H., 25
Palmerston, Viscount, 71
Parsons, Hon. C. A., 83
Paul's Cross, 43
Peckover, Dr. A., 39
Pennington, Sir I., 90
Percy, A., 40
Peterhouse, 36, 37
Pilkington, J., 89
Powell, Sir F. S., 16
Powell, W. S., 69
Powis, Earl, 21
Praeter, 91
Prior, M., 32, 63

REFORM, University, 80
Registers, 61, 62
Reyner, G. F., 16
Rickman, T., 8
Rowing, 102

ST. JOHN's Street, 16
Scott, A. J., 71, 72
Scott, Sir G. G., 15, 17
Scott, J. O., 22
Seaton, G., 55
Selwyn, G. A., 26, 103
Selwyn, W., 15
Seven Bishops, 58
Shittlecock, 101
Shorton, R., 40
Shrewsbury, Countess of, 5, 19, 28

INDEX

Sizar, 97
Smith, R., 50
Smith, W., 73
Snow, W., 102, 103
Stag Staircase, 4
Stage Plays, 23, 95
Staincoat, 5
Stankard, 5
Statues, 18
Statutes, 42, 43, 61, 74, 79, 81
Strafford, Lord, 18, 56, 62

Tatham, R., 22, 80
Taylor, B., 63
Taylor, C., 82
Thomas, Sir N., 25
Townshend, Marquis, 70
Trench, R. J. Le P., 102
Trinity College, 44

Tuckney, A., 57
Tutorial System, 77
Tyrrell, W., 26

Victoria, Queen, 18

Washington, Geo., 64
Whitaker, W., 48
Whitgift, J., 48
Whitworth, W. A., 105
Whytehead, T., 22
Wilberforce, W., 26
Wilderness, The, 9, 10
Williams, John, 7, 18, 25, 27, 28, 29, 52
Wood, J., 20, 78
Wordsworth, W., 25, 26, 32
Wren, Sir C., 7
Wren's Bridge, 8, 9

THE END

Printed by Ballantyne, Hanson & Co.
Edinburgh & London

Lightning Source UK Ltd.
Milton Keynes UK
UKHW010609210619
344792UK00001B/5/P